Successful Sunfish Racing

SUCCESSFUL SUNFISH RACING

Derrick Fries

John de Graff, Inc.
Clinton Corners, N.Y.
1984

© Derrick R. Fries 1984

ISBN 8286-0095-3
Library of Congress Card Number: 83-072325

No part of this book may be reproduced in any form by print, photoprint, microfilm, or any other means without written permission from the publisher.

John de Graff, Inc.
Clinton Corners, NY 12514

Book and jacket design by Laura Hough

First Printing

A portion of the material in Chapter 4 on reading the wind on the water originally appeared in YACHT RACING/CRUISING magazine.

Printed in the U.S.A.

Contents

ACKNOWLEDGMENTS   vii
INTRODUCTION   ix
1. THE SAIL AND RIG   1
2. JUSTIFYING THE JENS   17
3. THE DAGGERBOARD AND RUDDERS   27
4. READING THE WIND ON THE WATER   37
5. SPRINTING THE START   47
6. UPWIND   57
7. THE REACH   73
8. DOWNWIND   83
9. LESSONS LEARNED   91
10. ROLL-TACKING AND ROLL-JIBING   101
11. MAINTENANCE AND MOTHERING   109
12. THE PHYSICAL SUNFISH SAILOR   123
13. GARMENTS FOR SPEED   131
14. THE CLUBHOUSE   135
15. APPENDIX   137
    INDEX   145

Acknowledgments

Successful Sunfish Racing would not have been possible without the help of many generous people.

The friendly and kind members of Watkins Lake Yachting Association have given me much knowledge and support in the racing circuit. Their fleet is top quality with many sailors veterans of thirty years or more racing on the 250-acre lake.

My parents have been helpful in their loving and caring way in my pursuit of many personal goals. *Successful Sunfish Racing* is a small token of love and appreciation from me to them.

The Bob Pool family has been incredibly helpful in this entire project. Bob Pool, a distinguished plastic surgeon, has given me much objective insight into the overall intent of the book. He has devoted much personal time and effort developing and printing many of the photographs. I sincerely admire his fine personal character and terrific family. I dedicate this book to him, his wife Jackie, and children, John, Steve, and Marilyn.

Dave Powlison edited the manuscript for its benefit and my gratitude.

Finally, I would like to thank AMF Alcort for their cooperation and information. Jim Ronshagen and Lee Parks have helped greatly in making *Successful Sunfish Racing* a useful tool for Sunfish racers.

Happy racing,
Derrick Fries

Introduction

The Sunfish is truly an extraordinary racing craft. Its popularity is the result of its unique and simple design. Few other boats can be rigged in five minutes, carried to the beach, and raced. Sunfish racing programs have reinforced the intent of true one-design racing, and its history reflects that. The quality of Sunfish racers has made the boat a standout among single-handed classes. Great sailors such as Dave Chapin, Jeorg Bruder, Hans Fogh, Major Hall, Gary Hoyt, Gary Jobson, Carl Knight, Manton Scott, Will White, and many more emerged from success in the Sunfish class.

Another aspect of Sunfish character is longevity. A sail can last up to eight years and still be competitive. A hull, with proper maintenance, can last indefinitely, Scratches, patched holes, and color fade basically have no effect on speed. In this class, technology is blissfully ignored, and advanced equipment and continuous rig developments are games serious Sunfish sailors find irrelevant. Because the sole purpose of racing is to challenge the mind and body, there really is no evolution of the Sunfish; rather, there is an evolution of the body that sails it.

In this book, I provide insights into the advancement of modern Sunfish racing. I purposely omit in-depth discussion of tactics and rules, as other books thoroughly address these areas. This book's main purpose is the advancement of Sunfish racing.

During boat speed discussions, there are numerous references to body movement, or kinetics. Information is provided about the relationship of body kinetics to boat speed in regard to accepted body behavior in the class. No judgments are made about how the International Yacht Racing Union rules apply to these specialized movements.

The Sunfish has provided fun for thousands of families and individuals, both on the race course and off. May its success continue and prosper in the true spirit of one-design racing.

SUCCESSFUL SUNFISH RACING

The sail and rig. (Bob Pool)

1

The Sail and Rig

The main source of power for any sailboat is the sail, and the Sunfish is no exception. Questions about draft and fullness always arise, but in a Sunfish, differences in sail shapes and the effects of adjustments generally are overestimated. To prove this point, I raced the entire 1980 season—approximately 160 races in all types of conditions—without making a single outhaul adjustment, including racing and wave patterns. My sailing results and performance showed no changes from past years.

Such simplicity demonstrates that missing one wind shift is more costly than any minute change in speed resulting from sail adjustments. It is a mistake to become so involved in boat tuning that time is sacrificed on the water. Even the fastest boat on the course must start well and be in phase with the shifts to finish in the money.

When discussing sail trim, a problem arises when the Sunfish is compared to cat-rigged boats, such as the Laser and Force 5. This is an injustice, as the Sunfish rig and sail are unorthodox, and really only can be compared to other lateen rigs. One striking difference of lateen rigging is the incredible sail distortion created on port tack by the spars when the front sail section is pressed against the mast. In addition to this, air flow on the sail luff is greatly disturbed by the upper boom and mast, which necessitates a full entry and can leave the sail luff slightly scalloped, adding further to the distorted appearance.

When setting up the Sunfish sail, one of the first premises is that for all practical purposes, each sail is identical, although age and upkeep eventually will have some effect on shape. To understand positioning of the lateen Sunfish rig, visualize the triangle created by the sail and booms. As the wind increases, weather helm increases. To counteract this effect, the triangle must be moved forward. As the air lightens, helm decreases, and the triangle should be slid aft.

The two adjustment points for positioning the triangle are the gooseneck on the lower boom and the halyard attachment on the upper boom. Slide the halyard up and the gooseneck forward, and the triangle moves aft; slide the halyard down and the gooseneck aft, and the triangle moves forward. The tack always should remain just a few inches off the deck.

The proper range of positions for the gooseneck on the lower boom is between 17 and 21 inches aft of the tack. Position the gooseneck at 17 inches for drifters and at 21 inches for overpowering conditions. Outside that range, the boat usually is thrown off balance by excessive helm.

I never set the gooseneck bolt so tight that I can't slide the fitting on the boom. This allows me to adjust its location, even during a race, but only in light and medium winds. Offwind, the Sunfish is faster with the rig forward, so at the beginning of each offwind leg, I slide the lower boom two or three inches through the gooseneck, a maneuver that requires long arms and a fair amount of flexibility. To begin, I steer with fingertips to allow greater reach. I hold the mainsheet with my aft hand and use my forward hand to slide the boom forward. Then, to make the adjustment, I hook my two forefingers around the forward side of the gooseneck and grasp the boom with

Moving the gooseneck while under way requires agility and quickness. (Bob Pool)

my little finger and thumb. When I squeeze my hand together, the boom slides forward through the gooseneck. To ensure that the gooseneck remains positioned, duct-tape that section of the boom and then remove the tape, leaving a gum residue, which will prevent the gooseneck from sliding out of position. Taping must be repeated every ten races or so.

To slide the boom aft, for instance, when rounding leeward mark, I position two forefingers on the aft side of the gooseneck. With my thumb and little finger grasping the boom an inch or so from the gooseneck, I open my hand, pulling the boom aft through the fitting. If conditions change drastically during an upwind leg, you also may want to adjust the location, taking into account the current tactical and strategic considerations.

Tom Lihan, 1982 Laser North American champion, sails upwind with a full rig in the 1982 Championship of Champions regatta in Heath, Texas. Notice his crossed-leg hiking style, and the tape on the cockpit deck to prevent skidding. (Lee Parks)

For halyard location, the range is two to four inches, beginning at the upper end of the 10th segment and extending just into the 11th segment. (Segments are the spaces between the plastic sail clips, and are numbered from the tack up.) In light air, set the halyard at its lowest position, and as the wind increases, begin moving the halyard up the spar.

Another area of concern is the use of sail clips. In years past, it was common to see sails tied for the entire length of the upper and lower spars. Before this practice was ruled illegal, some racers even used high-poundage fishing line to tie off their grommets. However, it became difficult to assure an even distance between grommets, and today, only five grommets are tied off, replacing the standard plastic clips with one-eighth-inch, pre-stretched dacron line. Pre-stretched line virtually eliminates all stretch, so the sail can be set just as accurately as with stretchless plastic clips.

It is an absolute safety must to tie off the end grommets on the upper and lower spars. These are high-stress areas, and in heavy air, the standard clips may pop off. On the upper spar, grommets nine and ten are tied off to eliminate catching on the mast. One-eighth-inch line allows the grommets to slide freely, in contrast to the plastic clip, which must rotate around the boom with the sail.

On the lower boom, the second grommet should be fuller in front of the mast on port tack. A plastic clip pulls the sail too tight and produces distortion. By tying the sail approximately one and a half inches off the boom, air flow on port tack and the extra bag in the sail on starboard tack does not hinder air flow.

The standard metal S-hook on the sail tack also should be replaced with pre-stretched line, because in heavy air or during rapid luffing, the hook can be dislodged. To ensure adequate strength, the line must encircle the boom joint and tack grommet two or three times.

Pre-stretched line also should be used on the outhauls. For adequate purchase when adjusting the outhauls, an efficient rigging system is required. However, because there is not enough space in the last grommet for more than two one-eighth-inch lines, tie a small bowline around the clew through the grommet, and run extra purchase through that. Now the outhaul can be trimmed very

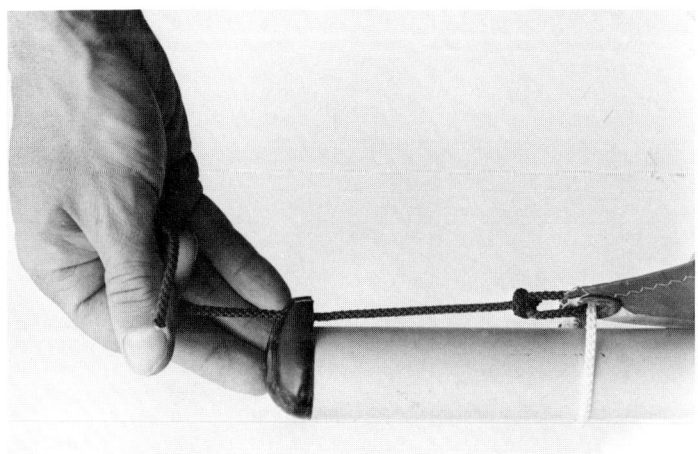

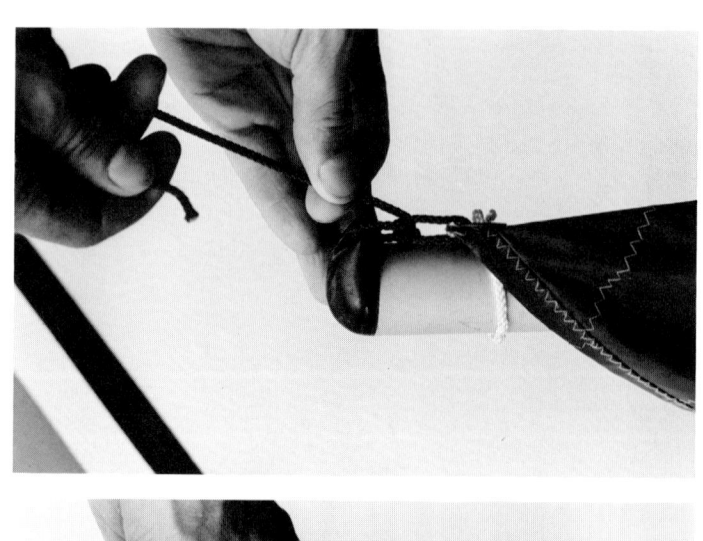
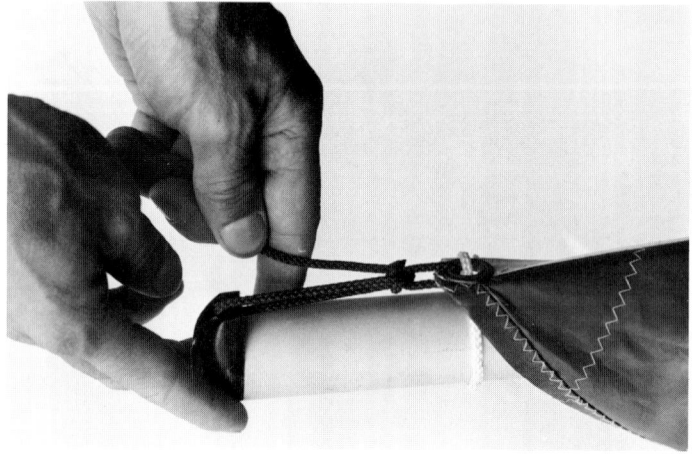
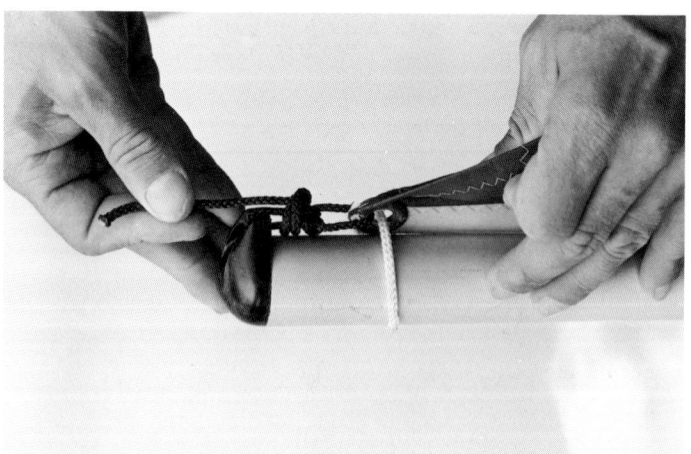

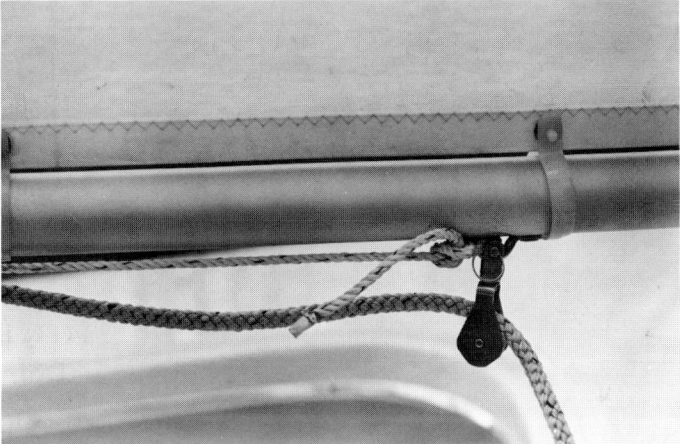

tightly, and you can be sure it will not stretch in heavy air.

Under certain conditions, you may need to make outhaul adjustments while on the water. Some sailors use an adjustable outhaul system utilizing a small cleat on the boom. But because the sail is equipped with plastic clips, clip movement along the boom is limited, and when trimming, the clips simply become caught along the boom diagonally. Because of this, adjustments are limited to one-quarter inch and only affect the last third of the sail. It is far better to adjust before or between races, when you have time to do it properly.

To adjust the outhauls on the water, you need three to five minutes and plenty of room for your boat to drift

Tying the outhaul with extra purchase can be very beneficial in heavy air. Removing the plastic clips here is a must. With adjustable outhauls, the bowline and extra purchase are also needed. However, the tail is simply anchored at the tack. Using ten feet of ⅛" pre-stretch the lower outhaul can be anchored at the forward boom pulley. The upper outhaul (20 feet long) can be anchored at the tack with a small bowline for extra purchase. (Bob Pool)

leeward. The steps are simple, but a bit of balancing is required. First, go head-to-wind and drop the sail. I prefer to drop it on the port side of the boat, which gives me more room to work on the deck than if I drop it on the starboard side. Technically, it leaves me on starboard tack, so while making adjustments, I don't have to be as concerned about the situation of port-starboard.

With the sail down, the outhauls hang about twelve inches beyond the transom. Since adjustments from that position are difficult, the second step is to remove the mast from the mast-step and lay it along the deck with the two booms. Be careful not to get the sail wet or—worse—to lose the entire rig overboard. Now, slide the whole rig forward approximately four feet; you should be able to reach both outhauls easily. If you have used extra-long outhauls, adjustment can be made at the tack for the upper outhaul and forward pulley block for the lower boom. You will still have to drop the rig to ensure that no plastic clips have hung up on the boom.

When adjusting the outhauls, check each plastic clip to ensure it has not become caught diagonally. If you wish to raise or lower the rig a couple of inches with the halyard, this too becomes an easy adjustment because the halyard on the boom is now at the cockpit.

With the halyard and outhauls adjusted, you are ready to raise the sail and begin racing again. However, there are still a couple of things to keep in mind. The boat will be drifting dead downwind. Before you raise the sail entirely, the boat must be turned 180 degrees, so that it faces head-to-wind. To turn the boat, raise the sail approximately three feet. The wind will catch the sail, and the boat should spin right around. Once into the wind, quickly raise the sail the rest of the way, being careful not to catch it on the tiller or mainsheet block.

One of the best places to adjust the outhauls is near the finish line. If the race committee is relocating after the start to finish the fleet at the weather mark, simply finish and sail back to the original starting area. Stay upwind of the line, and complete the outhaul adjustment there. If the finish line is fixed and will be the next starting line, sail upwind another 100 yards, then make your adjustments.

A common difficulty with the Sunfish sail is leech control. Sailors often comment on the wide variety of leeches. The first and foremost leech control is not the outhaul, but mainsheet tension. Because there is a close correlation between leech control and boat speed, the mainsheet also can be viewed as the boat's ultimate speed control. In all wind conditions, and particularly in light air, boat speed may increase or decrease as much as 20 percent with as little as two or three inches of mainsheet trim.

Leech control is a function of general mainsheet trim. Proper mainsheet trim is the key to speed in all conditions. (Bob Pool)

John Kostecki, 1982 Sunfish World Champion, sailing upwind in heavy air. He is using a medium-size Jens with a hard vang. Notice how flat the sail is with a proper looking leech. (Lee Parks)

Because the wind never blows in a straight line or in a constant direction, never cleat the mainsheet, but continually adjust it with each change in conditions. One sure way of keeping the sheet constantly alive is to forego mainsheet cleats. If you're accustomed to carrying cleats on the side decks, you'll find eliminating them also facilitates sliding fore and aft when surfing. On a Sunfish, as on many other single-handed boats, a good-looking leech is not necessarily synonymous with speed. During the 1978 World Championship Races in Puerto Rico, I drew a sail that looked equal to all the others, except for a leech that turned inside out whenever I sheeted hard while sailing upwind. I ignored the problem and simply concentrated on the shifts, and the sail showed no difference in speed.

Two other easily rigged controls are the JC strap and vang. The JC strap, named after its inventor John Christianson, holds the boom out when sailing offwind in light air and prevents unintentional jibes. The vang bends the lower and upper booms, pulling the draft out of the sail,

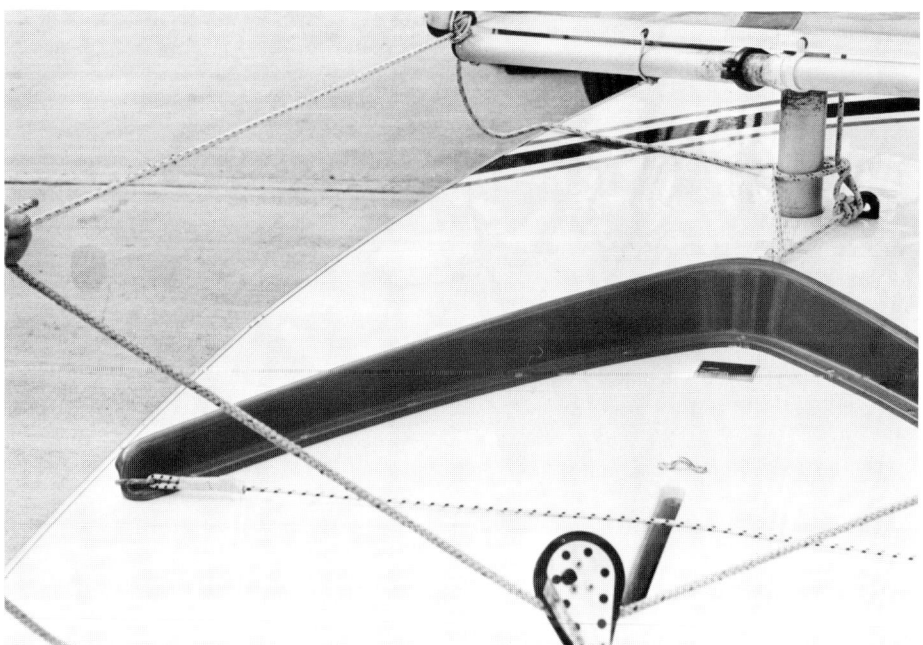

Proper use and rigging of the JC strap, used only in five knots or less. (Bob Pool)

flattening it. In addition, a tight vang makes sheeting easier. Since the JC strap and vang both require using the main halyard tail, only one control can be used at a time. Fortunately, they are used in vastly different wind conditions.

To rig the JC strap, secure the halyard around the cleat, leaving about 10 feet of halyard. Lead that line to the sail tack. With about seven feet of line remaining, tie a half hitch around the booms at the tack. Then run the rest of the line aft on the starboard side. That way, when rounding the weather mark, the strap will be positioned correctly, on the windward side. To keep the strap tail out of the water when not in use, tuck it under the daggerboard shockcord retainer.

This is the result of excess poundage from the vang. This skipper has bent the boom and torn the grommets out of the sail. Generally the maximum poundage for the vang is approximately 100 pounds of downward pressure. (Lee Parks)

The boom vang is rigged by running the halyard from the cleat to the base of the mast. Take several wraps around the mast with half hitches. The half hitches also should go around the halyard, as it comes down the mast. This keeps the halyard tight. From the half hitches, lead the line up to and over the gooseneck, between the boom and the mast, then back down through the main halyard eye and aft to the cleat. To tension the vang, push down on the bottom with one hand, just aft of where the vang

Proper tying of the vang is important. There is no need to go over the gooseneck more than once if using pre-stretch line. (Bob Pool)

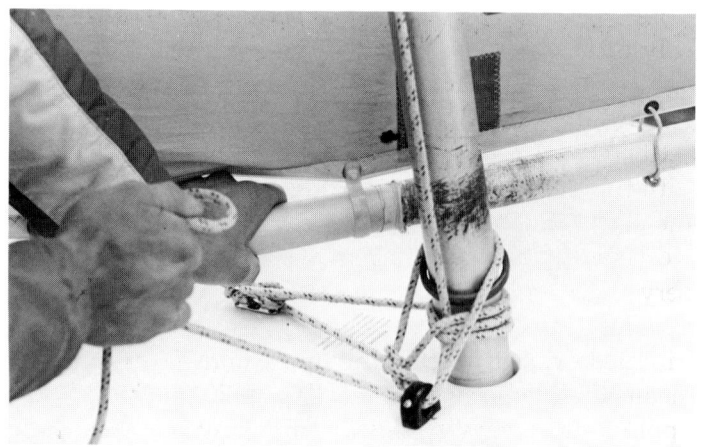

attaches. With your other hand, take up the slack created in the vang and secure the line to the halyard cleat. I've found it better to have too much vang than not enough, and when applying tension in heavy air I usually use about half my body weight.

The development of the Fogh sail has raised a question of maximum boat speed. When the new Fogh and the old standard, the Ratsey sail, are laid out on a flat surface, the Fogh is slightly larger, with a greater luff curve. Since the small tube sections of the Sunfish's upper and lower spars flex a great deal, the added luff curve is an advantage, for it better matches the spar bend. Because of its larger size, the Fogh must be sailed on both booms with more outhaul tension than does the Ratsey, but particularly on the upper boom.

Although the Fogh's fullness may be a minor disadvantage, its increased area more than compensates with better offwind performance. The Ratsey sail has grown with the class since its beginning, but the universal use of the Jens rig has demanded a sail with more luff curve. However, I still use my Ratsey regularly when sailing in very flat water.

To de-power the Fogh, the outhauls must be trimmed even tighter on the upper and lower spars. This means that very few or no scallops will develop along the upper spar. (Generally, in all wind conditions, the upper spar outhaul for a Fogh sail must be snug.) Mainsheet trim also must be slightly tighter. With a fat daggerboard and tight outhauls, the Fogh will consistently outperform the Ratsey.

The Sunfish sail at its best, upwind depowerized with a mini-Jens. (Bob Pool)

2

Justifying the Jens

The Jens rig is the newest innovation in modern Sunfish racing. Jens Hookanson pioneered the rig in the mid-1970s and proved its worth by winning the 1976 Sunfish North American Championship in medium and heavy air at Association Island, New York. Since then, the Jens has gained wide popularity at the World-racing level. Dave Chapin was second in the 1978 Worlds and won the same race in 1979 using a Jens rig.

The rig is based on a simple idea that narrows the upwind performance gap between lightweight and heavyweight sailors when the wind pipes up. In the past, a 130-pound sailor had practically no chance of matching speed with heavyweight competitors racing upwind in a breeze. A Jens rig reduces righting motion and produces a flatter, more aerodynamic sail, giving lightweight sailors an even chance in such conditions.

The efficiency of the Jens rests in its closeness to the deck, which eliminates much of the air flow under the boom. Aerodynamic tests have shown that reducing and/

Dave Chapin using a maxi-Jens at the 1982 Sunfish Worlds in San Francisco, CA. (Lee Parks)

or eliminating air flow under the boom helps lift considerably. With the boat's small daggerboard regulating sail shape, extra lift is precisely what is needed. The sail can be de-powered further, if necessary, by raking the upper boom aft, allowing the lower boom to run parallel to the deck and thus opening the leech. The Jens is especially fast upwind on starboard tack and is a favorite of racers who like to sprint away from the fleet at the start. Finally, because the rig is lower and further forward, the Jens makes balancing the helm offwind much easier.

The disadvantage of the Jens is that it is mainly a medium- and heavy-air rig, because the sail is much closer to the water. However, especially with the new, larger Fogh sails, the competitive difference between the Jens and a full rig is not particularly great. During one race, after a heavy-air first leg, the air lightened and I was

Dave Chapin attempting a tack with a maxi-Jens and a water jacket. (Steve Baker)

passed by a Jens-rigged boat skippered by a man only ten pounds lighter than I.

Another disadvantage of the Jens, especially for bigger sailors, becomes apparent when tacking and jibing. Because of the close proximity of the lower boom to the deck, roll-tacking and roll-jibing must be initiated earlier than is usual to allow the skipper to "kiss" the cockpit floor, thus avoiding a collision with the boom. Although tacking and jibing speed is impaired, upwind speed will compensate for the loss.

It is easy to rig the Jens. The only difficulty arises when placing the entire rig in the mast-step instead of simply hoisting the sail with the mast already in place. The job requires some upper-body strength. Follow these steps:

Step 1 Untie the halyard from the standard 10th or 11th section (sections are numbered between the plastic clips counting up from the tack). Re-tie it to the eighth or ninth section and tape the halyard in place on the boom. This is approximately 10 to 12 inches lower than the standard position. Its exact location will vary, depending on body weight and wind velocity. At 165 pounds, I have never sailed with the halyard below the ninth section. However, many smaller sailors are very fast at the seventh and eighth sections. The master of the Jens rig, Dave Chapin, usually sails with the halyard in the eighth or ninth section, and he weighs about 160 pounds. There are many variations of halyard position for different wind veloci-

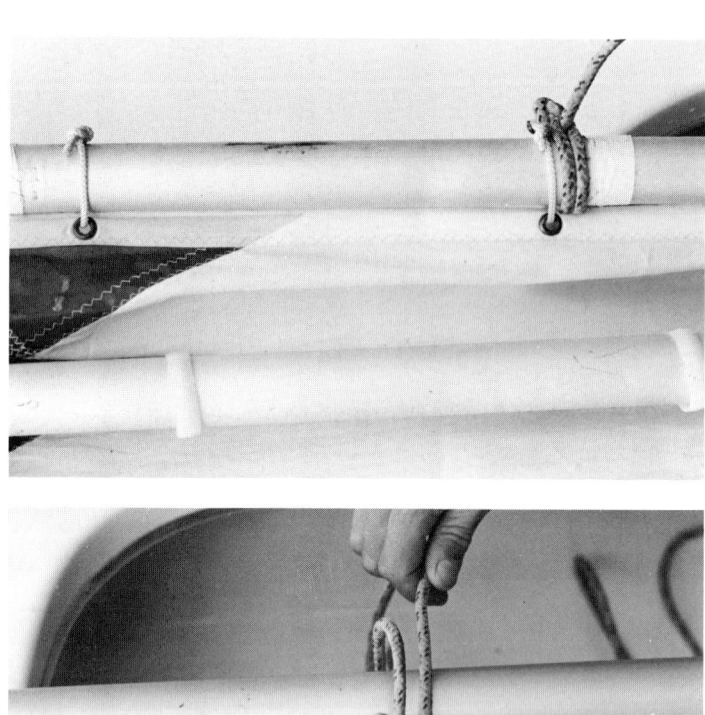

ties, but here are some benchmark figures to work from. In 20 knots of wind, a 145-pound skipper probably would carry the halyard 14 inches lower than the standard location. In the same wind, a 175-pound skipper probably would carry the halyard 10 inches below the standard position.

Step 2 Lay the mast alongside the upper boom.

Step 3 Using an oversized screwdriver to avoid damaging the screw head, loosen the gooseneck fitting and slide it

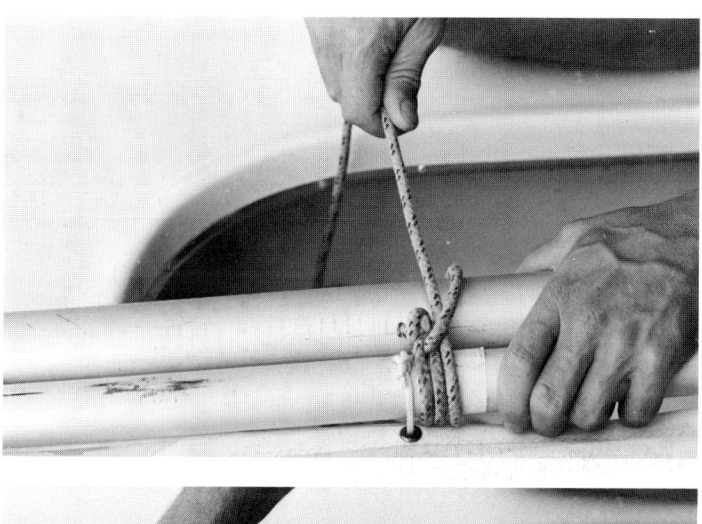

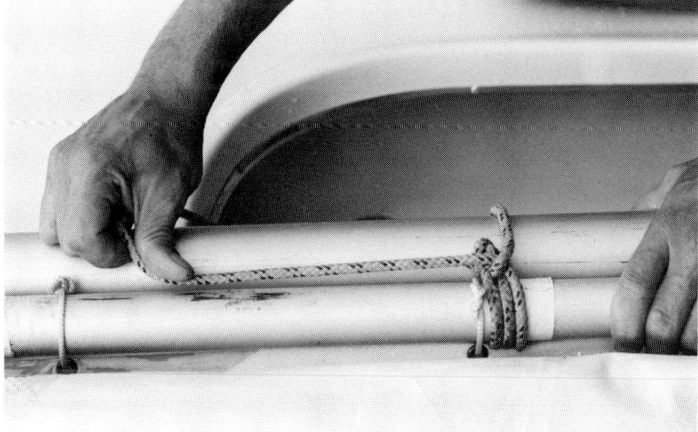

aft to a position approximately 20 inches from the tack. Like the halyard location, its exact position is relative to body weight and wind velocity, and the range is usually between 15 and 20 inches back from the tack.

Step 4 Take the halyard around both mast and spar, and then loop it through and over to make a half hitch knot.

Step 5 Put the halyard up and through the top of the mast, and bring the end back down.

Step 6 Make any final level of adjustments to the boom from the deck and pull the knot as tightly and firmly as possible around the spars.

Step 7 Grabbing both the mast and the upper spar, lift the rig into the mast-step.

Step 8 Shake the sail down to the desired level, then cleat.

Because class rules now allow an extra piece of line to be lashed to the upper spar against the mast, you may wish to modify the procedure described in Step 4. This eliminates the need for a half hitch in the halyard around the mast and upper spar.

Eventually, you may want to switch from the traditional rig to the Jens while on the water, perhaps between races. With practice, you should be able to make the change in fewer than five minutes. The most difficult step is standing the rig assembled in the boat. First, set the rig up on the deck, just as you would on land. Then lower the daggerboard all the way for stability, and make sure the wind is on the starboard beam, which will give you more room to work. To raise the rig, stand just aft of the splashboard for additional stability. Then, raise the sail as you would on land.

Rigging the Jens takes some practice. The halyard position is a key element. The halyard position here has been lowered only to a mini-Jens position. Notice the special halyard knot on the boom. The tighter the tension, the tighter it grips the spar. (Bob Pool)

Changing from a traditional rig to a Jens in the water is the single most difficult thing in Sunfish racing. One false move and you've created one horrible mess. Balance is more important than strength. At the 1978 North Americans I watched Paul Fendler, 135 pounds in three foot chop, do it with relative grace. (Bob Pool)

Learning to sail with the Jens rig is fun and easy. It is still a relatively new method and there are no universal rules about gooseneck positions or rig height. Experiment when possible, and spar with a friend. Eventually you will find the optimum settings for each wind condition, your weight, and your particular style of sailing.

The 1982 Sunfish Worlds, approaching the weather mark. The first boat is equipped with a small container hanging from the lower spar. Upon release, a protest flag will appear. (Allan Broadribb)

3

Daggerboards and Rudders

Sunfish daggerboards and rudders always have been the focus of controversy because there are several legal designs for each. Until 1972, all Sunfish featured U-shaped daggerboards and rudders. Although the daggerboard was a bit undersized, it did prove effective when sail trim and sailing technique were adjusted properly. However, the rudder had a distinct tendency to stall in heavy winds, making the boat a real handful to sail in a breeze, especially for recreational sailors.

In 1972 Alcort redesigned their daggerboards and rudders, creating the modern wing-shaped foils now found on the Sunfish. To improve heavy-air performance, rudder size was increased nearly 25 percent, but unfortunately, the already undersized daggerboards were made 12 percent smaller. The result was an immediate run on the new, larger rudders, while the old, U-shaped boards quickly became a valuable commodity among serious Sunfish racers.

Further clouding the picture, a third daggerboard was introduced by the Barrington, Rhode Island, Yacht Club. This one is three percent larger than the old, U-shaped boards and, like the old and new daggerboards, is perfectly legal.

The question of which board or rudder to use becomes even more complicated when variations in sail shape and design are introduced, since practically all adjustments made to the Sunfish are done to accommodate these underwater appendages. In addition, there are a number of fine-tuning methods that may be applied to optimize the performance of each.

DAGGERBOARDS

As more and more sailors raced and experimented with different daggerboards, it became clear that the bigger boards—the old U-shaped board and the Barrington board—had a definite edge over the new, wing-shaped boards. The logic behind this fact was brought to my attention in the summer of 1970 as I watched the legendary Carl Knight meticulously maintaining his daggerboard. He would remove it after racing to prevent the sun's ultraviolet rays from warping the wood or breaking up the hard epoxy paint. However, his rudder was sadly neglected. The rudder bottom and leading edge were not smooth, (it obviously had been scuffed hitting bottom or lying on the pavement prior to launching), and the paint was badly flaked and chipped. The contast between his rudder and daggerboard made no sense, so one day I asked Carl about this inconsistency.

"The rudder never remains in a straight line," Carl explained. "Thus, the rudder is used only in turbulent water. So smoothness there is not important. The daggerboard, on the other hand, remains fixed and flows through smooth, undisturbed water. There, the smoothness of the board serves a real purpose."

Carrying Carl's ideas about flow a bit further, I wondered if the surface of a Sunfish hull disturbs the flow of

The "New Board," "Old Board," and "Barrington Board." The Barrington has the greatest surface area and is the fastest of the three upwind. All boards are standing in the correct positions for the daggerboard trunk. The edge is placed forward (toward the bow) using the "new" and Barrington boards. The "old" board has the long edge forward for best overall performance. (Bob Pool)

water around the daggerboard. After all, sailors racing in heavy chop certainly experienced the pounding and banging of the hull on the waves, and older boats can "oilcan" in such conditions. In addition, the hull bottom between the mast-step and the daggerboard is always in motion, absorbing the shock of the waves—pushing the bow up and the stern down. Consequently, an even, or laminar, flow along the bottom of the hull hardly can be expected. Thus, the ideal board for all conditions is the one with the largest surface area—the Barrington board.

Another method of dealing with hull turbulence is to use a daggerboard of the maximum allowable thickness (2.0 centimeters). Pioneered by Carl Knight, the "fat board" allows greater speed and pointing, using a full sail for optimum power. Carl's board was so large it barely fit into his centerboard trunk. The additional thickness was achieved by wrapping the board with fiberglass cloth.

Besides making the board thicker, wrapping the board with fiberglass cloth has the distinct advantage of increasing its lateral stiffness. Such a board responds well to body kinetics, although on a much smaller scale than do boats with larger boards, such as Lasers. When done in a refined, smooth style, body movements transfer energy to the board, which, if stiff, will in turn pass accelerating energy along to the boat. Excluding body movement, a board with excessive lateral flex inhibits speed, because it stalls faster in waves, tacks, and jibes.

When applying fiberglass cloth and resin to a board, lay the cloth lengthwise to take advantage of its inherent stiffness. Use a quality resin, such as the Gougeon W.E.S.T. TM system, which is easy to apply, sand, and finish.

Assuming the Sunfish alters laminar flow when sailing through waves, a question arises as to which board shapes provide the greatest advantage. A boat going fast in the groove and steered straight benefits from a relatively sharp entry. Unfortunately, this is seldom the case with the Sunfish, which is more often than not sailed at the other end of the spectrum. As a result, a blunt leading edge with an elliptical shape and a tapered trailing edge that runs down to one quarter of an inch is as close as you can get to optimum, while remaining within class rules. This also saves the aft side of the board from damage by the daggerboard trunk.

To build up the leading edge, use quality marine filler, then glass over it to increase durability. When tapering the trailing edge remember that the maximum taper length is one and a quarter inches. Another factor critical to daggerboard effectiveness is the fit of the board in the trunk. Every sailor has sailed with a loosely fitting board and the accompanying daggerboard chatter. In addition, the board slops and twists in the trunk. All are deterrents to speed because they waste energy. The best solution is a fat board. I never have had a board chatter that was reinforced with fiberglass and resin.

To prepare the daggerboard trunk for the fat board, only minimal modifications are required. The majority of the work is preparing the board, and the main work on the trunk is ensuring that the trunk does not damage the tighter-fitting board. To be sure, vigorously sand all parts of the trunk. If you have not run the thickness of your board to the maximum, you may be able to fit in strips of anti-chafing tape, although it is decidedly preferable to build up the board instead of the trunk.

Regardless of how snugly you fit the daggerboard in the trunk, once it is wet it probably will slide up and down easily. To hold it in position, use a shockcord retainer. There are two methods of doing this. The first is to run a piece of five-sixteenths or three-eighths-inch shockcord from an eye on the upper forward corner of the board to the mast, halyard eye, or cleat. This works well, and if your board fits loosely in the trunk fore and aft, it has the advantage of cocking the board slightly aft. Another method is to rig a friction retainer. Use about two feet of shockcord with an eye at each end. Pull the shockcord across the deck to respectives sides, hooking it under the splash board. To rake the board aft simply place the shockcord on the aft-end of the board.

For years, a debate has raged about which edge should be the daggerboard's leading edge. In other words, how does this change in location of the board's center of effort affect performance? There is no exact answer to this question, because there are too many variables—wind, waves, body weight, and steering styles. But, when the results of major regattas are examined, we see that the Barrington boards perform best with the swept-back edge forward, while the old board sails best with the straight edge forward.

Often, sailors install new, untried boards prior to an important race or regatta. This can create difficulties if during the race the board suddenly begins to exhibit problems that were not experienced with the prior board. A better alternative is to use a practice board, saving the "good," thoroughly tested board for serious racing only. I have two practice boards—one for my "old" U-shaped board, and one for the Barrington board. In addition, I carry a "weed" board for inland lakes where weeds flourish. Such weeds destroy the leading edge from continuous clearing. By placing a quality marine tape on that edge, the board's life can be extended greatly. By painting the board white, I can easily view weeds.

The rudder in proper alignment with the hull. Having the rudder at 120 degrees will reduce rudder stall in heavy air. The cheeks on the rudder must always be tight. (Bob Pool)

Remember, the daggerboard is the key to boat speed. A one-degree warp in the board can mean the difference between 1st and 15th place. If you continuously monitor the condition of your board, it will more than repay you for your effort.

RUDDERS

As a youngster, I recall screaming along on a wild reach and suddenly having the rudder pop up. Later, as I began sailing in regattas, I often watched someone's rudder pop up and his boat go head-to-wind, careening into two or three other unfortunate skippers in the process.

To prevent inadvertent rudder kick-up, and to facilitate boat speed, there are a few small adjustments that may be made to the rudder. First, tighten the nut and bolt holding the rudder cheeks together. Even on new boats, like those used in the World Championships, the nut and bolt can work loose after an hour or two of heavy-weather sailing. When this happens, slopping and twisting causes it to steer more like a big keelboat than a lightweight Sunfish. To prevent this, score the bolt threads with pliers or add a double locknut. In addition, tighten the rudder-head cheeks so that two hands are required to raise the rudder when beaching or docking.

Loose gudgeons and pintles are also a source of rudder slop. Looseness indicates a need to reposition these fittings by filling the old fastener holes and re-drilling holes in the proper position. Slop also may develop because of wear, especially after four or five years of hard racing, at which point the fittings should be replaced.

Don't overlook the angle of the rudder in the "down" position. This varies from boat to boat, and the further aft the rudder is angled, the greater the weather helm and subsequent slowing. Make sure your rudder is angled as far forward as the class rules allow: "The angle from the line extending from the bottom of the hull next to the keelson and the leading edge of the rudder shall not be less than 120 degrees." (Sunfish class, rule 3, section rudder, c.)

The fourth race in the 1978 Worlds, held in Ponce, Puerto Rico. With winds gusting to 50 knots, many skippers had obvious problems with rudder stall. With a boat heeled to leeward and bearing off, rudder stall may occur in winds as low as 18 knots. (Steve Baker)

Other than using one of the newer, larger rudders, there is little to be done about the rudder's shape. As with the daggerboard, round the leading edge and round off the bottom. This allows the rudder to turn with less resistance. Sand the blade smooth and apply a good coat of varnish, or apply a saturation coat of resin to provide a bit more stiffness.

One final rudder-related item: make sure you have a good, universal-type joint between the tiller and tiller extension. Illegal until 1980, universals allow more versatile tiller movements without sacrificing feel for the helm. Prior to 1980, many ingenious methods were devised to obtain universal-joint results that were not actual universal fittings.

Kerry Klinger pioneered a method utilizing a long carriage bolt that allowed up-and-down tiller action as well as athwartship movement. Unfortunately, the bolt required a loose connection, which produced inferior feel for the responses of the boat and rudder.

With the advent of the larger rudder and the legalization of universal joints on tiller extensions, the Sunfish rudder has undergone much change since the 1960s. With a little more attention to detail, as discussed here, even better feel and speed may be realized.

Rounding the leeward mark at the 1981 Sunfish Worlds in Sardinia, Italy. All the skippers here should be doing intense water reading to determine their upwind game plan. (Steve Baker)

4

Reading the Wind on the Water

Every sailor knows that the wind never blows in a straight line, even over open water. And because most racing is done within relatively close proximity to land, the problem of variations in wind direction and velocity is increased. While meteorology has provided a fairly comprehensive theory of wind movement and has greatly aided long-term forecasting of wind origins in terms of velocity patterns and directional changes, it has not helped the average sailor much with the practical, immediate problem of what the breeze is doing 300 yards upwind.

Water reading provides a sailor with data on a short-term basis. It isn't difficult to understand the tactical advantage of knowing whether the wind ahead is going to veer, back, or change in velocity. Accurate water reading enables some people to always seem to be in the right place for a wind shift or a puff.

Reading wind on the water is like looking into the future. Many sailors spend a lot of time straining their necks looking at masthead flies, which, although valuable in some instances, are of limited usefulness because they only indicate what the wind is doing at one particular point in time. Furthermore, masthead flies only show what the apparent wind is doing 25 feet or so above the water. Reading the wind on the water not only saves your neck and deals with the true surface wind, but also tells you ahead of time what the wind will be doing when it gets to you.

The key to water reading lies in the composition of groups of waves, which I refer to as "wind groups." Because waves are a function of wind, the nature of their development serves as an indicator of both wind direction and velocity. To determine wind velocity, it is necessary to discern variations in color and shape of wind groups.

COLOR

All bodies of water undergo color changes that signify changes in wind strength. It is easy to read these changes in relatively "clean" water bodies: those that are free of both motorboat slop and pollution. It is the radiant blue hue of such water that enables the sailor to read wind on the surface easily. Water bodies that are characterized by a gray hue, most often lakes and rivers near major cities, are much more difficult to read.

Typically, a puff, or what I term a "positive wind group," shows on the surface of the water as a darker area, for instance, a deeper blue. Conversely, a color change that produces a lighter hue, possibly a silver, gray-blue, should be read as a lull, or a "negative wind group."

Variations of these positive and negative color changes will depend on the base color of the water in which you are racing. For instance, lakes of a brown color, characteristic of many of the central and southern states, will exhibit a brown or mud-hue color base. Thus, a positive wind group would be indicated by a darker brown area.

While watching for color changes during a race, it is important to remember that the rate of change will be determined by the mean wind speed. Therefore, a higher mean surface wind will create numerous color changes at a fast rate. This wind condition usually exists during the first twenty-four hours of a fresh northwester. Color and shape alterations can take place at such an accelerated rate that it is often difficult to assemble them into a meaningful pattern.

In contrast, a light, morning sea breeze may produce color changes that are extremely slow and almost hueless. With such minor differences in hue, positive and negative wind groups become much harder to distinguish. But for the trained eye, perceiving these changes mean huge gains on the race course.

SHAPE

No two wind groups are identical. As with snowflakes, the outward appearance may be basically similar, but closer examination will determine that the groups are all different. For the sake of simplicity, I have divided positive wind groups into three fundamental shapes: parabolic, linear, and irregular. Familiarity with these three basic shapes furnishes a framework for the more complex variations of puffs.

The parabola is the most commonly shaped puff on the water. It is normally associated with moderate-

Parabolic wind group. (D. Fries)

velocity winds from the west and the south. You will notice that a greater intensity of color is found at the center of the puff, thus signifying greater velocity deeper inside the wind group. Offwind, it's a tremendous advantage to be able to spot and get into such wind groups. Within the long, narrow-shaped puffs it is possible to sail one and a half times faster than will a boat that is sailing in a negative wind group.

Linear wind group. (D. Fries)

A linear wind group, or a wind line, is most commonly associated with sea breezes. But it is also found on inland lakes when the center of a high-pressure system is sitting overhead. Usually the lake is relatively flat except for one or two linear wind groups scattered about. Linear groups are normally larger in scale than are parabolic or irregular groups, and to the racer they usually mean larger gains or losses. In most cases, the first boat to sail into a linear wind group will make substantial gains, especially upwind.

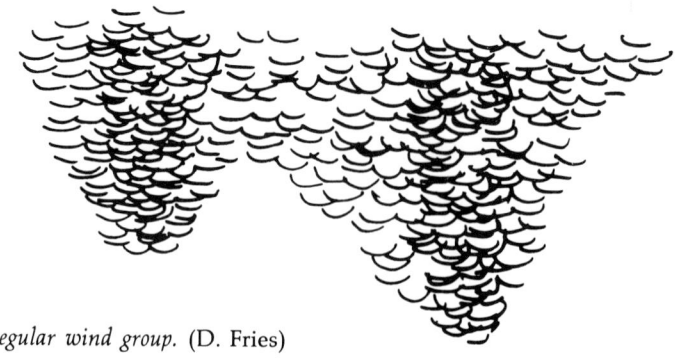

Irregular wind group. (D. Fries)

Irregular wind groups are distinguished by a basic absence of any definite, recognizable shape or pattern. In the spring and fall in North America it is not uncommon to sail a two-day series in nothing but irregular patterns. Because the puffs develop quickly, converging and diverging rapidly, a racer must be aggressive and on his toes to take advantage of such wind groups. If he fails to spot the development of these puffs soon enough, boat handling will be a considerable problem and the consequences may be disastrous.

Irregular wind group on a small inland lake. (D. Fries)

MOVEMENT

So far I have discussed only stationary identification of wind on the water. In addition to shape and color, a sailor reading wind also should be able to recognize and translate movement. For all practical purposes, the only factor that is permanent on a race course is change. When viewing a positive wind group, you must remember that its shape changes while it moves across the surface of the water. Often, after spotting a small, irregularly shaped

Reading the Wind on the Water · 41

puff, it will dissipate and become a negative wind group by the time you reach it. While this undoubtedly will be initially frustrating, with time and practice, you will be able to determine a logical, sequential pattern to wind movement and will learn to predict which wind group will be present when you reach a certain spot.

DIRECTION

With movement, all wind groups have a definable and predictable direction. Some puffs may deviate only a degree or two from the mean wind direction, while others may vary greatly. Given the proper conditions, an experienced water reader should be able to accurately identify the direction of a positive wind group, within a degree or two, up to two-thirds of a mile away. The advantages are obvious. Accurate reading of wind direction not only can help a sailor decide which side of the course to sail after rounding a leeward mark, but also helps solve the age-old dilemma of whether to tack immediately on a header or to keep going a little further, with the expectation that the wind will continue to head.

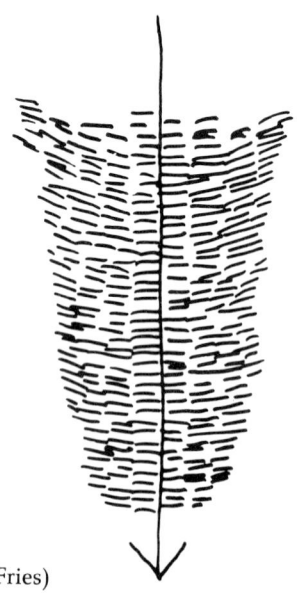

Direction in a parabolic wind group. (D. Fries)

There are two basic methods for determining wind direction in a puff. In a positive parabolic wind group, a mental line drawn vertically through the axis of the puff will indicate its direction.

Similarly, we can gain a rough approximation of wind direction, regardless of whether it's a puff or a lull, by visualizing a vertical line between wave crests. To the left and right of these directional axes, the wind should vary no more than half a degree or so. Notice in the wave group below that the wind on the right side is veered slightly and the wind on the left side slightly backed. Once a wind group is recognized and direction established, you can be reasonably assured that it will hold this direction until dissipation.

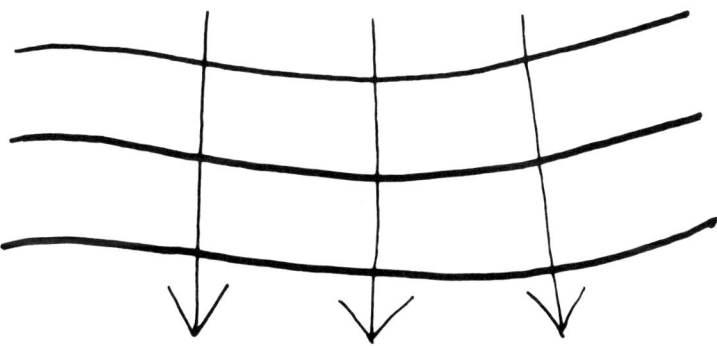

Wind direction in waves. (D. Fries)

PRACTICE

With practice, finding wind direction within a puff can become a split-second reflex. One good way to develop an eye for water reading simply is to spend some time drifting around on the water watching the wind and waves blow by. Try to spot the wind groups and forecast their strength and direction, and then wait to see if you are correct.

Another excellent method of familiarizing yourself with wind patterns is to study a body of water from an elevated vantage point such as a hill or a tall building. Even if you can't find a height to observe from, it is a good idea now and then simply to watch a race. Plant yourself a little downwind of the leeward mark and watch the proceedings. Watching other people utilize various wind groups can be tremendously educational.

OBSTACLES

Wind reading on the water, especially when determining direction, can be hindered by several factors. For instance, glare can distort wind patterns and water color and, at times, cause wind groups to appear to be positive when they actually are not. The obvious solution is to use good-quality sunglasses. A second factor that may confuse water reading is cross-chop, usually found on large bodies of water. The best way to deal with this problem is to learn to ignore the wave patterns left over from old wind systems. The new, positive wind group can be identified by watching the smaller, intermediate waves: not only will the waves be smaller, they will have a more defined shape.

RACE PREPARATION

Naturally, getting out to the race course early and checking the wind while observing the water patterns goes a long way to ensure recognition of positive wind groups during the race. To be certain, stand up in your boat before the race starts and carefully scan the water upwind to see if any changes have developed in the pattern, or if a significant wind group is coming that may affect the planning of your starting strategy.

Water reading is a little like reading a foreign language. Anyone can look at the writing, but only the person that has taken the time to learn the grammar and vocabulary can interpret and use what is written. The racing sailor who takes the time to learn the language of wind on the water will find that the skill will provide him with a tremendous advantage over the "uneducated" racer.

The 1977 Sunfish Worlds in Nassau, Bahamas. One hundred boats getting ready for the start. With a line this large, there is usually a huge middle-of-the-line sag. Will boat #841 clear the anchor line? (Bob Johnstone)

5

Sprinting the Start

The perfect start can make the rest of the race easy and fun. The real work, executing that perfect start, requires only three minutes of great concentration. A poor start, on the other hand, along with the ensuing catch-up strategies, may require up to ninety minutes of uninterrupted concentration. It's no coincidence that great racers are also great starters.

Typically, many Sunfish starts involve large fleets. Jockeying for position is challenging and exhilarating, and the boat has several atypical traits that should be considered. The boom is low and long, which means care must be taken not to get too close to another boat if you do not have right-of-way. The small Sunfish daggerboard necessitates a little extra room to leeward to get the boat going. Before the boat starts forward, it slides a bit more to leeward than boats with larger boards.

Much has been written about starting correctly. The ideas you'll find in other books have a number of general applications for Sunfish starting, but lack the necessary particulars. The variations are slight, but nonetheless important.

THE FAVORED END

One of the easiest and safest ways to determine the favored end of the starting line is the "mainsheet" technique, ideally suited for the Sunfish because of the boat's long boom and single-part mainsheet. With approximately seven to eight minutes before the start, when the fleet is large, and four to five minutes in a smaller fleet, sail down the line from the committee boat on starboard tack, steering for the pin. Keep the boat headed in a straight line. About two-thirds of the way down the line, trim the mainsheet until the sail is set just right for that point of sail. Put a mark on the sheet with a grease pencil or make a visual note about location of the sheet relative to where it exits from the mainsheet deck block.

The start of the fifth race during the 1978 Sunfish Worlds in Ponce, Peurto Rico. The right side of the course and committee boat end were favored here. (Steve Baker)

Next, round the pin and repeat the process, this time in the opposite direction. When you reach the two-thirds point, note the position of the mark you made on the first tack. If that mark is in the same location, the line is square. If it is now closer to the cockpit floor than it was on the first tack, the committee boat end is favored, and the air is to the right of the rhumb line. If the mark is between the deck block and the boom block, the pin end is favored, because the wind is to the left of the rhumb line.

Another method of checking starting line squareness suited to the Sunfish is the "friendship" start. This method requires two skippers of roughly equal boatspeed. At the eight-minute mark, both skippers start, one at the committee boat on starboard tack and the other at the pin end on port tack. Sail these tacks until it becomes obvious that one boat is clearly ahead, indicating the favored end. This usually only takes a minute or so.

In oscilliating, or shifting, breezes, caution and thought should be given prior to attempting the "mainsheet" technique or the "friendship" start in order to determine which phase of oscillation you are experiencing. To do this, watch the wind patterns on the water and take regular compass readings. A grease pencil is handy if you have a poor memory for compass numbers.

THE WARNING SIGNAL

With the ten-minute gun approaching, have two watches ready to go. Start the back-up watch at the warning, or ten-minute gun, and start the other watch at the preparatory, or five-minute gun. This way you're covered if one of the watches fails.

When the ten-minute gun is fired, you are officially racing. Focus the majority of the remaining time on strategy. Sail upwind to get a better vantage point on the weather leg. Standing up in the boat provides an even better view of the water, wind patterns, and distance to the first mark. Also watch the angles of boats sailing from the starting line, which should give you a better feel for the angle of the line and for the favored side of the course.

With seven minutes to go, make a preliminary decision about which side of the starting line is favored. Just prior to the preparatory gun, sail up to the committee boat and park next to it, sail luffing and boat motionless. If you can get there with five minutes and fifteen seconds to spare you'll have a front-row seat when the gun goes off and the flag is hoisted. You also may be able to hear the race committee counting down the five-minute gun, and make your time even more accurate. In addition, you will be in position to block others' view of the committee boat, and they will have to rely solely on the sound of the gun. Since there is a time lag between the point at which the gun is fired and when the report is heard at the other end of the starting line, the timing of your competitors may be thrown off.

PREPARATORY GUN

Now is the time to reconfirm the favored end of the starting line and to finalize your preliminary strategy. Keep a flexible attitude up to the three-minute mark in big fleets and the one-minute, thirty-second mark in small fleets. Unless you are in the final race and must defeat a specific boat, the location of the other competitors is irrelevant. Concentrate on your start. Make a final visual check upwind to identify the next wind oscillation, then sail the full extension of the line, past the pin, to help determine the line angle one more time.

As the countdown from one minute, thirty seconds begins, attention should be paid to a number of particulars. In contrast to other single-handed boats, the Sunfish's long boom facilitates good defensive strategy against luffs by other boats simply by letting the sail way out. This prevents prospective luffing boats from getting too close. Don't let the opponent even try to luff until he has an overlap. Too often, overtaking boats attempt to luff prior to an overlap. A warning usually curtails such behavior.

One move now used by many fine Sunfish sailors is the Barrett start, named after past Finn champion, Peter Barrett. This start is accomplished by obtaining a safe leeward position, which allows room to leeward to fall off and gain speed seconds before the gun. The Barrett start can be used at any location on the line, but the ideal starting spot is near the pin end. With about forty-five seconds to go in a big fleet, or with twenty-five seconds to go in a small fleet, make your final approach on port tack, cross-grain to the starboard-tack boats. Keep your eyes open for a hole to tack into. Once you have found a hole, tack into it and position your boat safely to leeward of the boats just up the line. If you tack underneath a group of luffing boats, luff right along with them without losing your access to open water to leeward. Be sure the next sailor coming up the line on port tack does not tack into your space. If this seems imminent, fall off, closing the hole, to discourage him. If you find boats up the line attempting to drive over you, fall off a little to gain speed and maintain your safe leeward position.

Often, when the fleet is large, the race committee underestimates the length of the starting line. Boats may begin lining up in rows as soon as one minute before the start. The Barrett start is not effective in such a circumstance, and the difference between a good and poor start rests in your ability to park the boat on the line. Because the Sunfish is lightweight and low freeboard, it has a tendency to drift down the line. Compensate for this and keep your boat on station, preserving a space to leeward to fall off into.

To park the boat on the line, heel it well to windward to reduce windage and place your boat in the leeward windshadow of your competitors. Luff the sail freely at all times. If a competitor attempts to luff you, make him sail out and around your long boom, a move that will put him out of luffing range. Luffing a mass of boats may be difficult. The key is vigorous verbal hailing. Hailing only the boat next to you is pointless, because the skipper must wait for the boat above him to move, and so on up the line. Instead, address the entire group, in particular, the boat farthest to windward. Demand they all come up together.

With the start nearing, prepare for your spring off the line. Often, skippers will become anxious, and a mass of boats will head over the line seconds early. When this happens, you must go with them. A general recall probably will be issued, and if not, the boats to weather of you may be called over individually. Your number may be hidden behind their sails, so cross the line with them early but inconspicuously. Keep your air clear, and your hull and sail hidden by the weather boats. If there are committee boats at both ends of the line, you may use the same screening manuever to leeward. The ideal screen is a boat that is not positioned lee-bow to you.

The race number and the number of premature starters are important to consider during a screened start. During the first races of a series, the race committee may want to set a precedent for the remainder of the event by calling as many boats over as possible and giving DNS's. However, if there are a large number of recalls, the committee may become anxious to get the race off, allowing a number of premature starters. Make sure you're among them.

With ten seconds left, cash in on your hold to leeward. Get the boat moving, gathering speed by sailing down the line, not forward across it. To do this, trim the sail and jab the rudder to windward, swinging the transom around. This maneuver places the boat perpendicular to the wind, in position for maximum acceleration.

With five seconds to go, you now have room to leeward as well as forward on the line. To ensure a maximum speed gain during this short period of time, bear off slightly, taking care not to head up before you have all the mainsheet in. At the gun, hike hard, head up, and you should squirt out in front of your competitors.

THE START

After the gun goes off and the race begins, what strategies guarantee further acceleration? In light air,

The start of race three at the 1982 Championship of Champions, at Rush Creek, Texas, a second or two after the gun was fired. All boats are on the line and charging. Boat #1 is very close to the pin. Notice the outhaul line running down to the tack. (Lee Parks)

some sailors nervously overtrim or, in heavy air, oversteer through the waves. Neither strategy is good, because energy always should be directed in a productive manner. To continue your spring off the line, and during the first third of the weather leg, concentration and body movements must synchronize. This skill separates the good racer from the great one. Sail by feel and observe other boats and their tacking angles. This can slow your boat, but the ability to switch from "automatic pilot" to "manual control" is a necessary skill that must be mastered.

The use of body kinetics is crucial directly after the start. The five percent speed increase gained by utilizing body weight can mean the difference between being sandwiched in the masses or being the first boat to tack on a new wind oscillation. In light air, a smooth fluid body

The start of race two at the 1982 Championship of Champions. The committee boat has a large number of boats there, however, the left side of the windward leg proved to be favored. (Lee Parks)

move may facilitate passage through marginal lee-bow situations. In heavy air, an extra-hard hike may be necessary to blast away from a group of competitors.

Right after the start, a Sunfish competition is like a drag race. The vast majority of boats will sail on starboard tack for the first 100 yards. You must have clear air and be ready to tack if you suspect a significant oscillation has occurred. Many times, the ability to tack on the first shift can pull you right away from the fleet. As a general rule of thumb, assume that heading your boat in the right direction is more important than is clear air. This is not to say that you should sail in everyone's backwind for the first 100 yards. However, in marginal situations heading in the right direction will usually afford the greatest gain. Chances are good that many sailors are not aware of wind oscillations at the start. They will look to other boats for clues about wind direction. This often occurs at the start when an oscillation favors port tack and the left side of the course is favored.

Consolidation and clear air at the start also are important factors. Shortly after the start, you probably will want to tack onto port, especially in a substantial oscillation. Do so, but be careful not to sail too far, or more than 30 boat lengths, from the fleet. Now tack back onto starboard and stay with the fleet on the favored side of the course. This requires a fairly substantial oscillation at the start, favoring the port tack.

Inevitably, you will make a wrong decision about the favored end of the starting line. Being buried at the start is difficult, and recovering can be a chore even for the best of sailors. After a poor start, you have to beat the others at their own game. Taking a flyer is not the answer. Learning to ignore the other boats and sailing smart is. Keep your air clean and sail in the proper direction on each of the following legs, maintaining a positive and optimistic mental attitude. Your adrenaline will flow, and you will sail that much harder. The goal is to sail the remainder of the race mistake-free. You may have committed your major mistake of the regatta, but many of your competitors soon will be making mistakes, upon which you can capitalize. If one of the leaders is keeping an eye on your progress, noting the number of boats you are chewing up, you may have an added psychological edge. Your chances of regaining ground increase as the race goes on, especially on upcoming weather legs. Then, the problem of clean air lessens as the fleet spreads out.

From a race committee boat, it is possible to observe an entire series of good starts. You'll view the gamut, from light to heavy air, from aggressive to passive starts. When the fleet is large, you'll be amazed at the scope of mid-line sag and at the strategies the good racers employ to ensure a good start. Keep a note pad handy—there are so many variables it will be impossible to remember them all. Even if you remember only a few of the things you observe, your next start will be much improved.

(Bob Pool)

6

Upwind

When sailing upwind, the vast majority of sailing craft are symmetrical, performing just as well on one tack as on the other. The Sunfish is an exception to this rule. On port tack, the front portion of the sail is pressed against the mast, but on starboard tack it is not. Because of this, the boat must be sailed upwind differently on each tack. It is around this difference that all discussions of upwind sailing must be centered.

Photos A and B demonstrate the correct upwind form on starboard and port tacks. The photos were taken only moments apart and the air velocity was the same in both pictures. Note that on port tack, mainsheet trim is much tighter. This is standard for all wind conditions, except light air. To make the distinctions clear between sailing in light air versus heavy air, let's examine each condition separately.

(A,B) Port and starboard proper upwind style. (Bob Pool)

LIGHT AIR

Photo C shows the boat well balanced upwind. Note that the skipper has placed himself in the cockpit to keep the boat heeled slightly, better balancing the helm. He is not resting on the cockpit floor, but is kneeling, better prepared for a sudden roll-tack or a quick move out of the cockpit should the wind velocity increase.

(C) Light air boat balance. (Bob Pool)

Photos D and E show that upwind in 10 knots the skipper is relaxed and, most important, maintains a neutral helm. He uses his body to balance the boat and he situates himself even with the forward edge of the cockpit. There is no reason to sit any further forward, although in chop you may want to move aft a few inches to raise the bow and prevent bow plunges.

Light-air steering is very delicate. It is done with a light touch of the thumb and fingers, through which you should be able to sense the water flow around the rudder. Through his fingers, an excellent sailor instantly can detect just one small piece of seaweed caught on the rudder. Equally obvious are abnormal lee or weather helm developments. In light air, the wrist is used for minor tiller adjustments. Heel should be increased in chop to prevent waves from coming over the deck and to allow the hull to knife through the water. The Greater Detroit Sunfish Association's annual Greater Detroit Sunfish Regatta is held on Lake St. Clair, which, because it is shallow and hosts much motorboat traffic, evidences some of the choppiest seas in the world. Sailing correctly in such conditions requires continually playing the mainsheet to steer the boat. When a series of waves approaches, bear off slightly by sheeting out, and the boat will pick up speed and power. When a flat spot appears, sheet in slightly. The boat will head up and pinch, usually one or two degrees at most. During these manuevers, limit mainsheet adjustments to three to five inches, and course changes will amount only to about four degrees.

(D) Eight knots port tack. Notice that the tight sheeting provides excellent drive. Boom flex is a result of this snug sheeting. The body is compact.

(E) The Skipper has found a puff in about six knots of air. Flex the forward leg and lean out at the waist. (Bob Pool)

One common technique that increases light-air speed is capitalizing on body shape. Contrary to downwind sailing, the body acts as a speed inhibitor in lighter air. Loose clothing, such as hoods and bulky jackets, absorb increased windage and reduce speed. Although these affects are small, every element adds up. Think of your body as one tight, compact package. Keep your arms close to your torso and make mainsheet and tiller adjustments at elbow level or below rather than from the shoulders. Notice the compact body style in the light-air photos.

MEDIUM AND HEAVY AIR

In medium and heavy air, port tack is faster and provides a better angle of attack than does starboard tack. Many times, in heavy air, I have tacked from starboard to port just to increase speed and to improve my angle. In some instances, in very heavy air, I have planned my final leg to ensure that I will be on the faster, more powerful port tack as I approach the finish line. The Jens rig is an exception to this rule when used in heavy air. The Jens de-powers the sail, decreasing daggerboard stall, and equalizes speed on the two tacks.

Body movements are not as compact in heavy air as in light air. Now gross motor movements must come from the shoulders and plenty of torque is recommended when pulling in large quantities of sheet. Shoulders are curved less because weight must be moved outward to balance the boat.

Photo F shows proper form upwind in approximately 18 knots. The skipper is in a good position and has the boat trimmed perfectly. The outhauls have been tightened on both spars, with more tension on the upper spar. The gooseneck has moved aft from 18 to 21 inches, measuring from the tack of the sail. To reduce weather helm, the boat is sailed slightly flatter than it would be in light air. Mainsheet trim is increased to put the boom almost over the end of the transom.

The gentle, guiding technique used in light air is quickly replaced with aggressive and vigorous steering

(F) Blasting upwind with a flatter sail and tighter sheet tension. The skipper, although relaxed, is hiking spread-eagle style for good boat balance. (Bob Pool)

movements as the boat is muscled through the waves. Hold the extension firmly, with the handle between the first two fingers. Instead of steering with the wrist or elbow, use a combination of elbow and shoulder movement while trimming and easing the mainsheet with the opposite hand.

To make the boat respond to small changes in wave patterns, steer at a faster rate. To facilitate necessary meanderings through the waves, tiller and body motions must be abrupt and strong. You must place the boat on the proper position on the wave. Irregular or gross tiller movements slow the boat very little.

As you head up over the crest of a wave, trim the sail and head up slightly, swinging your upper body aft. For example, on port tack, the right arm pushes the tiller away from the body while the left arm trims the mainsheet. As you come off the back of the wave, the process is reversed. In this way, your arms and upper body move continuously, maximizing efficiency. Stay in full control; never let the boat sail you.

Hiking upwind in medium and heavy air is frequently overdone. Many sailors make the mistake of hiking 100 percent over the entire leg. Few are in adequate physical condition for this. Other legs of the course also require hiking, and speed will be sacrificed if you burn out on the weather legs.

Hiking should be done in two stages—power-on, or flat out 100-percent hiking, and power-off, which is a semi-comfortable hiked position.

The most efficient hiking method is the semi-droop, or power-off hike. This method of hiking is done from the legs not from the stomach. During a power-on hike, the

Holding the tiller properly can be very critical when blasting upwind in waves. The palm of the hand should always be facing down. (Bob Pool)

Semi-droop upwind. The mainsheet can be used for support for the upper body. Notice that in all photos, the mainsheet is never cleated. (Bob Pool)

body becomes more horizontal, transferring stress to the stomach. In power-off, the sailor is in a relaxed, semi-droop hike. Because the boat is low to the water, a full-droop will drag the skipper in the water, slowing the boat.

The photo opposite demonstrates a power hike. The skipper is wearing a water jacket, and his position makes it evident that a power hike cannot be maintained over an entire weather leg. For extra stability, I wedge my aft foot between the deck and the bottom of the storage compart-

Power-on hike, rounding the weather mark in 20 knots. The skipper is working to keep the boat flat and speed up. Loss of speed and excess heel will create rudder stall here. (Lee Parks)

ment, with my heel in the drainage groove. This connects me firmly to the boat and transfers the energy of my movements directly to the hull.

As the tactical mind of the middle-distance runner performs 100 percent during certain points of the race, so must the mind of the power sailor perform during a number of key race points. These are the power-on stages:

1. The start. All energy is focused on producing maximum speed to power away from the fleet.
2. Tacking. In heavy air especially, each tack is followed by full hiking until boat speed is restored and flow around the board achieved.
3. Mark roundings. Because of the quantity of traffic, this area of the course requires maximum effort to pass other boats.

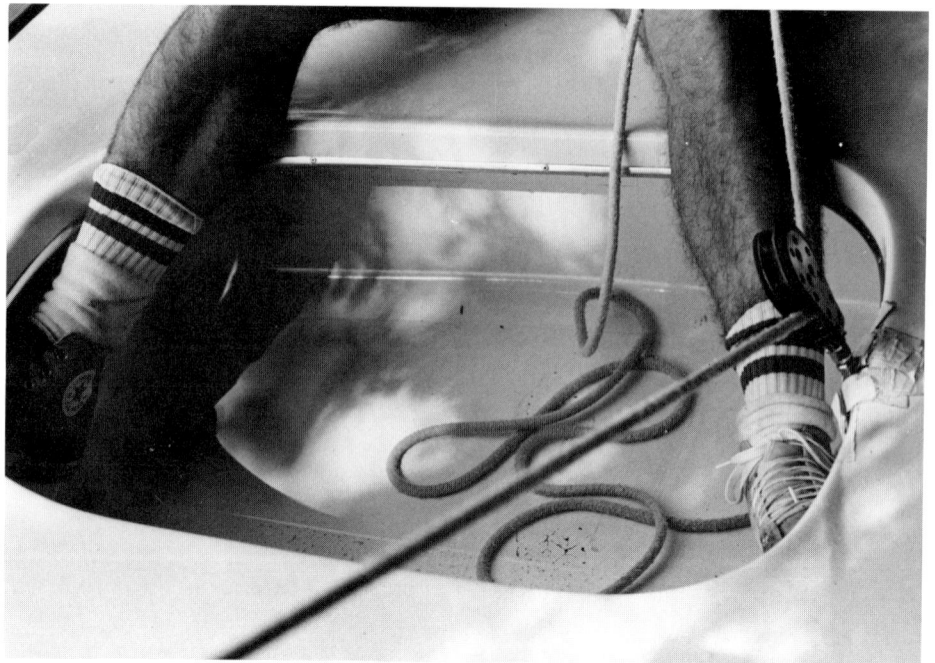

Hiking style upwind. This technique may vary with leg length. The aft foot is wedged into the cockpit storage area for better boat control and leverage. (Bob Pool)

4. Lee-bow maneuvers. When attempting a lee-bow maneuver in medium and heavy air, a full hike prevents sliding into the windward boat's bad air.

5. Puffs. Hiking at full capacity in puffs keeps momentum up, and overpowers those who allow their boats to heel over or to luff excessively.

6. The finish. During the last 200 yards in any race, competition is fierce for valuable places. This is where the sailor makes his "kick" and where, when the fleet is large, the extra ounces of energy expended can bring big awards.

In heavy air, some classes of boats, such as the Laser and Force 5, benefit from raising the daggerboard a bit as wind velocity increases, reducing heeling and increasing boat speed. Unfortunately, this technique is not effective

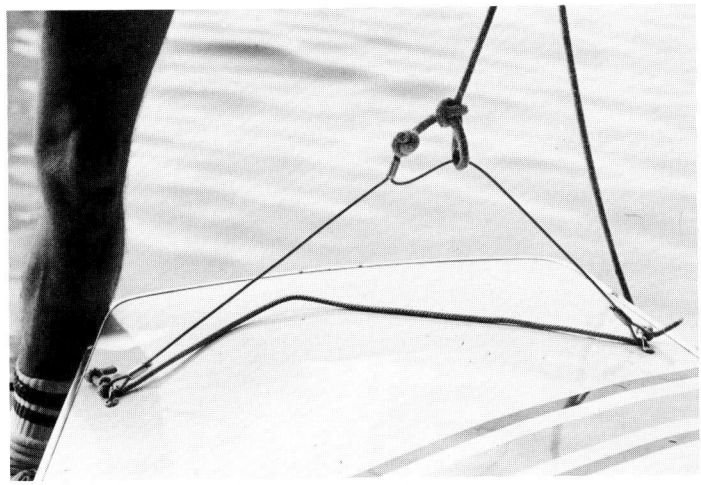

One of the many varied positions for the bridle. Here it is set at approximately eight knots. (Bob Pool)

with the Sunfish. During the fourth race of the 1978 Sunfish Worlds at Ponce, Puerto Rico, a forty-five-minute squall occurred shortly after the start. With gusts approaching 50 knots, I thought the time ideal to raise the board a bit. I raised it about five inches and quickly found myself slowing and losing boats. Similarly, raising the board in drifting conditions also is ill-advised.

During the 1973 Worlds competition held in Martinique, I noticed some unique sailing styles. Very distinct was the style of 140-pound Pierre Siegentheler, who compensates for daggerboard sideslipping by sailing the boat with a pronounced heel. Siegentheler's method provided several advantages. First the chine of the boat digging in the water acted like a longitudinal daggerboard, similar in principle to many boardless catamarans. Second, the reduction of wetted surface increased speed. Finally, heeling made hiking more effective because his body no longer dragged through the water. The only drawback of Siegentheler's method was its negative effect on pointing ability. Despite this, Pierre won that year's Worlds, and repeated in 1977.

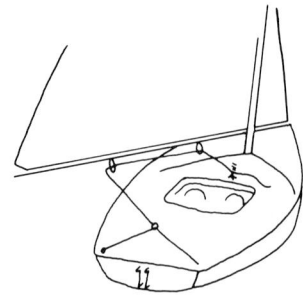

WIRE BRIDLE
0–5K

CENTERED

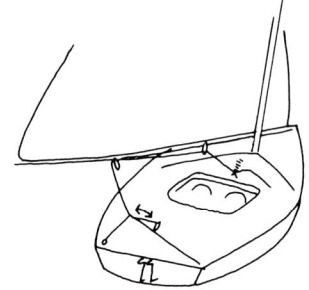

WIRE BRIDLE
5–10K

PORT SLIDE
3"

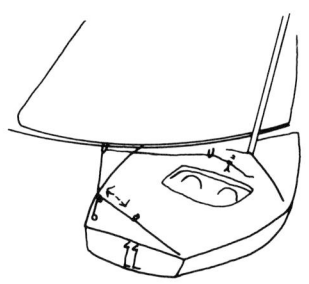

WIRE BRIDLE
10–15K

PORT SLIDE
FREELY

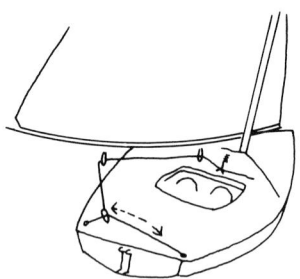

ROPE BRIDLE
15K+

PORT/STARBOARD
SLIDE FREELY

Port/Starboard heavy air position, 31" rope, bridle sliding. (Bob Pool)

Most of the techniques mentioned here are true for both the port and starboard tack. In general, port tack allows tighter sheeting and better boat speed. Starboard tack requires extra-hard hiking and slightly less mainsheet tension. Here is a summary of upwind strategies. (See also page 143.)

THE PRINCIPLES OF UPWIND SAILING

I. LIGHT AIR

1. BOAT SPEED
    A. Reading the water
    B. Playing the shifts
    C. Choosing the correct course

2. ANGLE OF HEEL
    A. Eight knots or less—10-degree heel
    B. Reduce heel in puffs
    C. In short choppy waves, increase heel to cut through the water
    D. Never sail completely flat

3. **MAINSHEET TRIM**
    A. Slow sail-trim adjustments
    B. Use thin diameter line (Ex. ¼" 0–6 knots)
    C. Use wrist and elbow to trim only
    D. Use fingertips on mainsheet for better feel
    E. Trim harder on port than starboard: port—over corner of transom; starboard—2–4" past corner

4. **PROPER WEIGHT-POSITIONING**
    A. Fluid body movements
    B. Use body to aid in steerage
    C. Flat water—forward leg even with forward edge of cockpit
    D. Choppy conditions—forward leg 2–4" aft of forward edge of cockpit

5. **STEERAGE**
    A. Use your fingertips
    B. Smooth precise movements
    C. No more than 15 degrees tiller movement from centerline

II. MEDIUM AND HEAVY AIR

1. **BOAT SPEED**
    A. Reading the water and waves
    B. Playing the shifts
    C. Choosing the correct course

2. **ANGLE OF HEEL**
    A. Five-degree heel in mean wind speed
    B. Reduce heel in puffs
    C. Sail flat in flat water
    D. Slight heel in rough water

3. **MAINSHEET TRIM**
    A. Powerful mainsheet trims
    B. Use thick diameter line (Ex. ⅜")
    C. Use shoulders and arms to make adjustments
    D. Use hand on tiller for firm control
    E. Trim harder on port than on starboard: port—2"

inside corner of transom; starboard—over corner of transom

4. PROPER WEIGHT-POSITIONING
   A. Aggressive body movements to help power through waves
   B. Center of the cockpit in all wind above 14 knots
   C. Use V-hike with lower legs to better balance body
   D. Semi-droop hike

5. STEERAGE
   A. Use your hands and fingertips to steer
   B. Jabbing tiller motions to help position the boat in the wave
   C. Up to 25 degrees movement from centerline
   D. Raise tiller to make jabs and gross tiller movements easier

Blasting along on a good reach. Weight displacement for flat water is mid-cockpit. (Bob Pool)

7

The Reach

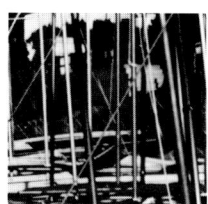
Blasting along on a screaming reach can be one of the most rewarding facets of Sunfish racing, particularly when passing other boats. While on a reach you can easily predict your competitors' tactical moves and, unlike upwind sailing, boats can not split and sail in various directions. Here utilization of wind shifts is of minor importance, and making up yardage with extra speed is crucial. Maximum speed here is achieved with a combination of techniques that change with conditions.

In light air, sail the boat delicately. In most instances, rudder movement for steerage is not necessary and inhibits speed. Good light-air reaching form is shown on page 74, where the skipper is carrying a neutral helm and the boat is heeled to windward. Besides creating a neutral helm, such heeling reduces the wetted surface and traps air, producing extra sail area. This kind of sailing requires a transition from the techniques utilized during other legs of the course. If you can think of the rudder as a fixed assembly you won't be tempted to use it to change course.

Neutral helm and plenty of windward boat heel. This reduces wetted surface and helps neutralize helm. (Bob Johnstone)

Having fun with sparring partner, John Pool. Sparring partners can be very important in determining speed and working on objective tuning techniques. (Bob Pool)

Attempting to use the rudder to change course will slow the boat.

There is a common misunderstanding about this type of steering. Body steering must be done over a long distance. Short-radius turns cannot be effective using body language without slowing the boat. To understand how much control you have without using the rudder, practice steering on a reach without touching the helm. Better still, take your rudder off, secure it in the cockpit or on the deck, and try reaching. Initial steering without the rudder may be frustrating, but with time you'll get the hang of it and your offwind speed will increase. Many college and junior sailing program use this type of exercise during routine training.

When steering with your body, all movements must be graceful and smooth, because sudden movement disturbs the flow around the rudder, daggerboard, and sail. Catlike motions are required in winds up to seven knots; in stronger winds, more pronounced movements are necessary.

To achieve maximum boatspeed in heavy air, a different approach is required. At approximately 10 knots,

1980 Sunfish Worlds in Aruba. Wild reaches are the trademark of the Caribbean. This may also mean saltwater in your eyes. (Steve Baker)

body steering becomes ineffective, and marginal planing conditions develop. When the boat begins planing, it becomes very stable, largely because of its flat bottom. Now gaining speed requires full concentration and great sensitivity because the boat cannot be muscled through the waves as on upwind legs.

Plane right away and maintain your plane for as long as possible. Involvement in tactical maneuvers with other competitors, or in housekeeping details, is a sure ticket to the back of the fleet. Keep the boat flat, give the mainsheet a couple of quick pumps when a puff hits, and you'll be off.

To help maintain planing, keep your eyes on the wind on the water behind you. Stay in the puff, bearing

The skipper has moved weight forward and worked the boat to catch this wave. Notice he has trimmed the mainsheet slightly. (Bob Johnstone)

off as you gain speed and heading up as wind velocity decreases and the boat slows.

With increasing wind come bigger waves. In waves, the Sunfish becomes more than a sailboat—it is now a sailboat as well as a sailboard, with two power sources: the wind and the waves. The boat's flat bottom makes surfing possible on even the smallest of waves. The photos on pages 76 and 77 show the stages of catching a wave. As the wave approaches, the skipper moves forward, lifting the transom. At this point the wave is moving faster than is the boat. To increase speed, preventing the wave from passing under and by the boat, give a couple of quick pumps to the mainsheet. From this point, concentrate on keeping the bow positioned at the lowest

To keep the bow up, he has rotated his upper body aft. The boat is in full acceleration here. The boat is now heeled slightly to windward.
(B. Johnstone)

point of the wave. Many times, this means steering across, rather than down, the wave. On a broad reach or run you can make up ground to leeward while maintaining good speed.

Getting the boat up to speed as the wave approaches is important. As mentioned, two or three quick mainsheet pumps will usually do that. Rule 60 of the International Yacht Racing Rules prohibits rhythmic pumping of the sail but allows up to three pumps to get the boat surfing down the face of a wave.

Because the Sunfish has tremendous surfing ability, the class is more permissive about kinetic interpretations than are other classes. However, knowing the exact language of Rule 60 is important, and you must be sensitive to the potential consequences of your actions.

The surf is now near its completion. The skipper should be looking for the next wave. (B. Johnstone)

Although it is wise to avoid sailing up the back of a wave, there are times when you must. Weight must be shifted aft to allow the bow to lift easily over the wave. If you pump the sail and rock aft and to windward simultaneously, a few extra ounces of forward momentum will be gained. Once through the wave, keep the bow aimed toward the low points or troughs, a strategy that should prevent having to drive through the backside of more waves.

Occasionally, you may find yourself slipping up the backside of a wave. To avoid this, plan your steering strategy in advance, always looking ahead a few waves. Your angle of attack may vary as much as 30 degrees, but the boat will continue to go fast, and you won't find yourself stopped dead by a wall of water.

To further enhance planing, particularly in marginal conditions, keep your air clean. The lack of a few grams of air may make the difference between going fast or slow. Sail in the puffs as much as possible. In lighter air, keep the boat heeled slightly to windward to reduce wetted surface and keep the helm balanced.

Mike Catalano is one of the wizards of offwind sailing. In light to medium air, he uses the smallest wave to his advantage by placing his forward knee against the forward edge of the cockpit rim. Both feet are placed firmly on the cockpit floor and his body is at the center of the cockpit. With perfect timing, he flexes his forward leg against the cockpit rim and pushes aft, a powerful flex starting in his stomach muscles and running through his entire leg. Coordinating his movements with a sail pump and slight rock to windward makes Mike an offwind terror.

In very light air, Mike adds an extra weapon to his speed arsenal. Upon approaching a boat on a reach or run, he starts a warm and friendly conversation with his opponent, usually making him laugh. This breaks the opponent's concentration and movement from the laughter disturbs air and water flow. As the opponent's boat speed diminishes, Mike quickly blankets and passes him, continuing the conversation to reduce the agony of being passed.

SAILING ON REACHES

1. If you plan to attack on the reaching leg and to pass many boats, get upwind into the passing lane. This strategy works especially well on long reaches that are 90 to 110 degrees to the wind. Avoid intruding on a skipper's "social space" when passing, or you may end up in a luffing match.

2. Except when planing, keep the boat heeled to windward to balance the helm.

3. In light air, steer the boat without moving the rudder.

4. In heavy air, significant amounts of steering help maintain a surf.

5. Slide the mainsheet to the end of the bridle on both starboard and port reaches.

6. If you have water in the cockpit, use the reaches to drain.

7. In medium to heavy air on reaches of 120 degrees or more, trim the mainsheet directly from the boom block. In light air, do this on points of sail greater than 90 degrees.

8. When rounding the windward mark, boat position and speed are more important than equipment adjustments.

9. Slide the gooseneck slightly aft for speed and helm balance. Repositioning should take less than four seconds.

10. Generally, sail up in the lulls and down in the puffs.

11. If a competitor is attempting to pass you windward, a sharp luff and a verbal hail will discourage him.

12. When demanding room at marks, always address all of the boats hindering your safe and seamanlike rounding.

13. Roll-jibes at the jibe mark or on runs are as important as roll-tacks upwind.

14. To ride waves, use fore and aft weight displacement. Move forward down the wave and aft over the top of it.

15. On the second reach, note any changes in the mean wind direction. This enables you to set your game plan for the next beat.

Chris Friend, showing excellent downwind form at the 1982 Sunfish World Championship. Chris has the boat heeled properly to weather and is holding the mainsheet from the boom block. (Allan Broadribb)

8

Downwind

 Downwind sailing techniques are an extension of those used on the reaching legs. Applicable here is an aggressive attack on the wind and waves.

The Sunfish is easy to handle downwind because of the stability provided by its flat bottom. If you have doubts about the boat's stability, a short sail in a Laser or Force 5, particularly in a breeze, will prove this point. One of the best training techniques for sailing a Sunfish is to spend time on a faster and less stable boat, such as the Force 5. After the Force 5, the Sunfish will feel like a toy, both upwind and down. In fact, many of the class's finest sailors also race other boats such as Finns, Lasers, and Force 5s.

Because downwind sailing is the slowest point of sail for the Sunfish, more race time is spent on this leg than on reaches. Therefore, learning how to sail this leg well is important.

A unique attribute of the Sunfish is its ability to sail by-the-lee. Generally, sailing by-the-lee reduces the number of jibes downwind, and a properly performed jibe can be a great sailing move. Often, however, an extra jibe near the leeward mark can be costly. When sailing by-the-lee, you can go as far as 195 degrees off the wind while maintaining speed and making good your course to leeward. For this, you'll need an extra-long mainsheet, approximately 28 feet.

To attack downwind, you must use your body. Body movement turns the boat and allows it to ride across a wave. The fore and aft movements work your overgrown surfboard around to catch the finest wave. Lean windward to bear off and lean leeward to head up. As on other legs of the course, specific techniques vary from one wind condition to another. Let's take a look at the two major categories.

Jim Owen showing good light air form. Mainsheet is out approximately 90 degrees to centerline of boat. Jim crosses his legs for balance. He also is hand-holding the mainsheet for the boom block. Notice his simple dagger board retaining device, tight elastic rubber between the splashboards. (D. Fries)

LIGHT AIR

One of the few opportunities you have to attack well in light air comes when there are relatively large waves, which allow you to surf. Because of the boat's slow speed, it takes a lot of effort to get on a wave, and equally as much to maintain the ride, but if you are successful you'll be moving faster than your competition.

Another point of attack materializes when you run into large wind oscillations. Occasionally, oscillations will vary as much as 20 degrees. Jibe if you receive a significant header, but in relatively steady air, tacking downwind is not productive. Generally, tacking downwind means more than three tacks.

However, the most important attack is superior boat speed. To maximize speed in light air:

1. The sail should be 90 degrees to the centerline of the boat.

2. Sail with only as much board as needed. However, never pull the board up all the way, for that causes water to boil in the trunk opening. The board should at least fill the daggerboard trunk. A reference mark on the board helps assess its position.

3. As on reaches, balance your helm. Neutral helm keeps boat speed up. Heel the boat to weather, both in and out of waves, and use body movements to help steer and/or make minor course changes.

$A = 12$ BOAT LENGTHS - $0{-}5K$
$B = 8$ BOAT LENGTHS - $5{-}10K$
$C = 5$ BOAT LENGTHS - $10{-}15K$
$D = 3$ BOAT LENGTHS - $15 + K$

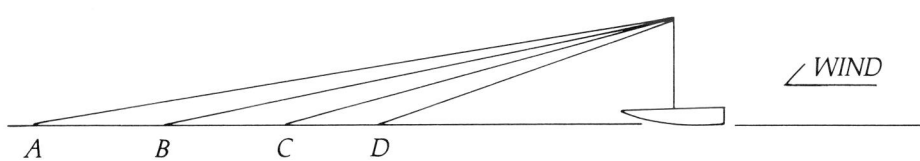

4. Move gracefully. Jerky movements inhibit speed.
5. Unless sailing a small course, avoid luffing matches.
6. In a dying breeze, when approaching the leeward mark move to the inside. This is particularly helpful if a logjam of boats develops at the mark.
7. In winds between three and seven knots, carry your vang snug. Don't use the vang in less than three knots.
8. If you require extra speed to establish or break an overlap, a slight rock to windward is usually acceptable.
9. Sailing by the lee as far as 15 degrees is allowable for short periods of time.

HEAVY AIR

In heavy air, the same principles apply as in light air, but they are modified slightly. It is critical to use waves efficiently, and more aggressive body, sheet, and helm movements are necessary to remain synchronized with the waves. To attack in heavy air:

1. Keep the bow at the lowest section of the wave and prolong the downhill ride by steering with the rudder. Steering across the wave also may be necessary.
2. When going up the backside of a wide, shift body weight aft. When going down a wave, shift it forward, near the daggerboard area.
3. Through big waves, keep the board at least one-third of the way down to assist in tracking across waves.
4. Keep the vang tight.
5. For better response and feel, trim the mainsheet directly from the boom.
6. Except when surfing down a wave, heel the boat to windward.

7. For better stability, spread your legs apart to opposite vertical cockpit walls.
8. Never intentionally sail through a wave.
9. Surf in clean water, free from other competitors' quarter waves when possible.
10. Jibe only when accelerating down a wave. Then there is less force on the rig, and the chances of capsizing are reduced.

After turning the weather mark and heading downwind, be sensitive to wind and water conditions and sail immediately for the favored side of the course. The decision to steer to the left or right of the rhumb line is determined by wind velocity and direction. However, also keep currents and water depths in mind because shallow water may mean bigger surfing waves and current may affect speed.

LEEWARD MARK ROUNDINGS

Setting up well for the leeward mark provides many opportunities. Generally, at least a 145-degree radius turn must be made, and because such a turn consumes energy and time, mistakes can occur. Learning to capitalize on others' mistakes can prove the biggest tactical advantage of the race.

In a pack of boats, an ideal leeward-mark rounding is not always possible. Then, your goal must simply be to stay inside to achieve better boat speed. In heavy air, many sailors either overshoot the mark or fail to sheet in fast enough, creating an opening between themselves and the mark. Take advantage of these situations.

In the past, much has been written about proper rounding of marks and many diverse techniques are accepted practice today. Here are some general tactical rules of thumb to remember when competing in large fleets.

1. Establish your overlap well ahead of time, as much as 7 to 10 boat-lengths from the mark. This will

Wild mark rounding leads to a great show for spectators. (Lee Parks)

cause the outside yacht to give you plenty of room to make a smooth rounding.

2. Stay to the inside and demand room.

3. When gaining on a pack of boats, swing wide in anticipation of many boats overshooting the mark. If so, chances are you'll be able to take the inside route.

4. In heavy air, do not try to establish an overlap once you reach the two-boat-length circle. At this point, things are happening too quickly for the overtaken skipper to comply.

5. In heavy air, use long sweeping motions to gather the sheet as you turn. Start trimming the sheet just prior to your course change and use your steering hand to collect the extra sheet. You'll also find that it is easier to gather the sheet when you are surfing down a wave.

6. When approaching the mark inside on port tack with a herd of boats you may be forced into a bad turn. To avoid this, counterattack by jibing onto starboard about 10 boat-lengths from the mark. Sailing by the lee if necessary, force your competitors to swing wide with you. This maneuver works best in light and medium air.

7. Prior to rounding the leeward mark, plan your strategy for the next weather leg. Preplanning enables you to round the mark prepared for your next move.

8. When rounding the mark in medium air with a clearly established inside overlap, make a safe and seamanlike rounding, gaining an extra half-boat length on your competitor and hogging a little extra room.

9. If you want to tack immediately after rounding the leeward mark and sail to the left side of the course, an absolutely tight mark-rounding is necessary. If, by chance, someone has a slight inside overlap on you, round the mark and pinch him off as you trim in on port tack. This should cause him to bear off and will free you to tack. If he instead decides to tack, immediately tack on him, taking his air and forcing him back to the right side of the course. Then sail the favored side in accordance with your game plan.

The first phase of the important roll-tack. (Bob Pool)

9

Roll-Tacking and Jibing

In light and medium winds, roll-tacking and roll-jibing a Sunfish can provide an extra squirt of speed that will pull you through the maneuvers at full speed. These techniques are a unique blend of science and art—for every action there is an equal and opposite reaction, and the ability to move through the tack or jibe fluidly and efficiently is an art.

Generally, the speed of the roll increases with wind velocity. For instance, a drifting roll-tack or jibe may take as many as five seconds, while the same maneuver might take as little as three seconds in a 15- to 18-knot wind.

Five-to-ten-knot winds and smooth water are optimum conditions for learning roll-tacking and jibing. Such conditions enable you to closely monitor which of your movements work with or against the wind. Not having to deal with waves allows you to concentrate more on your movements.

When first attempting roll-tacks and jibes, you may feel very awkward—as if you are going to fall out of the boat. However, with practice, these feelings will subside.

(Step 1) Tiller never turned more than 45 degrees. (Bob Poole)

(Step 2) Begin to heel boat with body. (Bob Poole)

ROLL-TACK

To roll-tack the Sunfish:

Step 1 With the boat heeled slightly, as it should be in light and medium winds, use your weight to gently pull the boat level.

Step 2 As soon as the boat is level, begin gradually

(Step 3) Sail has now lost air, boat heel will be easier now. (Bob Poole)

(Step 4) Using the legs for support, bend at the waist. (Bob Poole)

pushing the tiller about 45 degrees to leeward, using a full arm extension.

Step 3 Utilizing your weight, heel the boat to windward, using enough force to keep the sail full. Slide out and aft to keep the bow from digging into the water.

Step 4 As the boat reaches head-to-wind, there should be about 20 degrees of windward heel. I know when I've rolled the boat far enough to windward, because the seat of my shorts takes a quick dip in the water.

(Step 5) Recovering and getting under the boom smoothly is important. (Bob Poole)

(Step 6) Sail is now driving good, boat is at greatest heel. (Bob Poole)

Step 5 With the boat just beyond head-to-wind, bend at the waist and grab the cockpit rim on the opposite side of the boat. This helps maintain balance and provides a handle with which to pull yourself to the other side of the boat.

Step 6 With the boat on the new tack, pull yourself across the cockpit, ducking the boom and pivoting on the balls of your feet. Always face forward when crossing the cockpit, as this allows a better feel for the boat's direction and keeps you aware of the position of the rest of the fleet.

(Step 7) Boat is accelerating, body movement must be smooth. (Bob Poole)

(Step 8) Hand exchange must be completed before sitting down. Can not let go of tiller or mainsheet. (Bob Pool)

Step 7 Now comes the most challenging part of the maneuver—the blind mainsheet hand exchange. Start by transferring the mainsheet to the tiller hand, so that for a moment that hand is holding both tiller and mainsheet. At this point, both hands still have a grip on the mainsheet.

Step 8 With both hands still holding the mainsheet, release the tiller hand. Then, with the hand that was holding the tiller, reposition your grip so that you take the sheet directly from the mainsheet deck block.

The hand exchange is quite crucial. Neither the tiller or the mainsheet should be dropped. To rotate without twisting the mainsheet in the legs, take the mainsheet to the tiller hand. This will allow a free hand. Same thing happens when adjusting gooseneck. (Bob Pool)

ROLL-JIBE

The roll-jibe is fun and exciting, and when performed with good technique it can be accomplished in strong winds. The key to success is getting through the jibe with speed equal to or better than that attained just prior to initiating the roll. Basically, the roll-jibe is a roll-tack in reverse, with less tiller motion because you steer with more boat heel.

The motion on the roll-jibe can be kept to a minimum when following these steps:

Step 1 Determine correct conditions in relation to wave and wind.

Step 2 Heel the boat to weather in a gradual motion. Down a wave and in a lull when possible.

Step 3 At approximately 20-percent heel, turn the tiller to leeward about 10 degrees.

(Step 1) Determine correct position strategically.

(Step 2) Heel boat to windward increasing speed.

Roll-Tacking and Jibing · 97

(Step 3) Rudder is making a minor adjustment to lee.

(Steps 4 & 5) Maximum boat heel during jibe.

Step 4 Pull the main across in one big sweeping fashion. (Caution should be given to make sure that the daggerboard has been pushed down slightly.)

(Steps 6 & 7) Recovery, standing up to do hand exchange.

(Step 8a) Must be very smooth when sitting back down.

Step 5 Remain on the windward side of the boat until the sail has crossed the centerline. (The recovery stage, like the roll-tack, will begin.)

Step 6 Grabbing the windward cockpit rim, recover by standing up.

Step 7 Exchange the mainsheet using the blind mainsheet hand exchange and rotate on the balls of your feet, facing forward. Never rotate toward the stern of the boat.

Step 8a & b Sit down gently, neutralize the helm again by heeling the boat to weather. Caution should be given not to overturn the boat! Many skippers make tiller adjustments that are too large. This slows the boat and creates a longer sailing distance to the next mark.

The roll-jibe is a fun and exciting procedure. Boatspeed can remain constant. The speed of the roll-jibe is like that of the roll-tack. Drifting conditions will mean a slower procedure while medium conditions will mean doing things at an accelerated rate.

(Step 8b) Heel boat to leeward smoothly again, and neutralize helm. (Bob Pool)

10

Lessons Learned

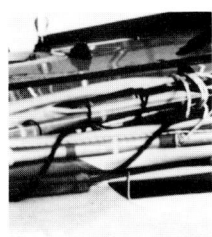 Each regatta, regardless of size, offers something to be learned. The ability to remember what went right or wrong, and why, makes these lessons particularly valuable. What follows are five important lessons I have learned on the race course.

SURVIVAL OF THE FITTEST

During the summer of 1971, the North American competition was held in Sayville, New York. The regatta was sailed in predominantly light air and at sixteen years of age, my inexperience was offset somewhat by both lightwinds and by my light weight. Because the regatta was sailed in high heat and humidity, fatigue and mental alacrity were important performance variables, although many sailors appeared undaunted by the heat and the long hours in their boats. For others, the difficult conditions created havoc, because they were unprepared for the heat and became impatient. The winner of the regatta, Jack Evans, demonstrated tremendous patience and experience under adverse conditions.

I placed seventh at the North Americans, and qualified for the 1972 Worlds, which were held in Bermuda. There, heavy air and big seas provided exciting racing—conditions quite the opposite of Sayville. During the third race, I rounded the leeward mark with a lead of about 10 boat-lengths, but when I started back upwind, I was tired. At that time, class rules allowed unlimited weight to be worn by skippers. Fatigue from carrying about 70 pounds impaired my ability to think clearly.

Bob Bowles, who won the race, passed me like a destroyer on his way up the second weather leg. As I approached the second weather mark, I was extremely tired and fell into third place. I mistook a spectator boat on the starboard side of the course for the committee boat, assumed I was on the third weather leg, and tried to finish. I was disoriented and could not believe the race continued further. I had sailed way past the weather mark and was very frustrated.

LESSON: Charles Darwin formulated the theory of survival of the fittest, and this philosophy is applicable to man's various sporting contests. The fittest, physically, emotionally, and intellectually, survive as winners. At both Sayville and Bermuda, the winner was best suited and prepared for the contest. Jack Evans showed unmatched patience and the ability to change gears readily. He adapted to difficult conditions in a smooth and natural fashion. Bob Bowles displayed intelligent sailing and used his great physical strength to excel. He had no equal in terms of the ability to adapt quickly to the conditions. Both men truly were well prepared for the environment —they had trained for the conditions, and their efforts were transformed into victory.

THE VALUE OF DETAILED NOTETAKING

During my days of collegiate sailing, I had the opportunity to travel to many sailing sites throughout North America. This experience was enjoyable and very enriching. One classic autumn racing series is the Timme Angsten Regatta, held at Chicago's Belmont Harbor. Schools from all over North America qualify to compete on the icy Lake Michigan waters, where Lehman 10s are sailed with both skipper and crew. The harbor exists next to many multi-story buildings. When the wind blows from the west, it swirls around the buildings, often diverging on the small harbor. Belmont Harbor has its own peculiar and characteristic conditions, and can seem illogical to the inexperienced sailor. Complicating the situation are the swells that come through the mouth of the harbor, creating a small current.

During my freshman year, I observed the Angsten races while other, more practiced members of our team participated. As a sophomore, my experience was bewildering—I was sailing, but could not manage consistent results, and I became confused dealing with the windshifts. As a freshman, I had compiled a series of notes on the wind's peculiarities at Belmont. These notes should have helped me as a sophomore, but I was still missing a key ingredient. Although my notes listed general conditions about the boats and about current and wind movements, I needed to make some key changes before I could be successful in my junior year.

LESSON: Shortly after leaving the harbor as a sophomore, I reflected on my experience. My boat speed was very good, near the top 20 percent. However, my ability to sail in the right direction was near the bottom 20 percent. While this was the first time I had ever had the opportunity to observe conditions thoroughly before racing, the notes from my freshman year were of little help.

During the drive home, I realized I needed to make a dramatic change in my notetaking method. I had been recording general information, not specific details, about wind conditions. What I needed was a log of every race that would detail wind velocity, current, direction, temperature, air mass, and course. I also needed to note the favored side of the starting line and every weather leg.

My sophomore year proved a good time to start making detailed notes, as the wind blew from all quadrants with varying velocity. With twenty races in three days, my log would take some time, and I needed to start right away before the memory of the race faded.

The results my junior year were tremendous. My log provided the ability to anticipate wind changes, which proved a terrific edge. In the last ten races, I finished in the top five. I rose from 16th rank in A division my sophomore year to first place as a junior.

During the course of a lifetime of sailing, the chances of sailing on the same body of water more than once are great. Often, annual events are held at the same location, so detailed notetaking can be valuable.

IMPROVING THROUGH OBSERVATION

The Winnetka, Illinois, Yacht Club hosted the 1970 Sunfish North American Championships. Many great Sunfish sailors were on hand—Carl Knight, Ted Moore, Chuck Millican, Major Hall, Will White, Larry Lewis, Tom Ehman, Bob Bowles, and others. The first day saw light air, but for the remainder of the series, winds were between 10 and 20 knots—ideal sailing conditions. At fifteen, I felt very green and had a lot to learn.

Each sailor had his own particular style. In the first race, I followed Dick Griffin up the first weather leg. I had sailed against Dick before, and considered him fast and intelligent. At 130 pounds, his upwind speed in medium air always fascinated me. He hiked hard and sailed brilliantly through waves, cutting each with grace and speed. In this qualification race, we finished first and second in what was generally light air.

As the series progressed and the wind's velocity intensified, my performance gradually faltered. During the fourth race, I examined Ted Moore's style with analytical care. He wore a large number of sweatshirts, and his aggressive upwind style and tacks made him unbeatable. I learned from observing him never to place myself in a defensive position on the first weather leg. A hard, charging offense is the key to getting to the weather mark first.

During the fifth race, I went with Carl Knight to the left side of the course in an offshore breeze of 18 knots. In his quiet manner, Carl sheeted hard and ever so slightly pinched a little further to windward. His pointing ability was unmatched. Offwind, he pumped the main, holding the sheet from the boom block to achieve better feel for the boat and sail. I was impressed with his uncanny ability to read windshifts.

LESSON: With so many great sailors on hand, it would have been foolish not to observe carefully. Although every sailor has his own style, each style has much to offer the inexperienced sailor. Many times while going upwind I would attempt their techniques. Offwind, they showed perserverance while playing the waves and keeping the boat on a plane for the longest possible time. Ashore, I would question them individually about methods they used on the water. This was informative, and they were helpful. Observing great sailors and their habits can be invaluable, and imitating their styles may be one of the quickest ways to learn how to race well.

LIGHT-AIR METHODS

During the 1973 Sunfish North Americans at Devils Lake, Michigan, there was much to be learned about sailing in light air. After the first two races in medium air, I had a small overall lead. The wind was steady and showed slow oscillations, and I adapted to this easily.

The second day brought a light, puffy wind. Consistent results would be the key to holding the lead, but it was not uncommon for sailors to gain or lose 30 boats on one leg. Wind velocity was spotty, and puffs would appear and disappear irregularly. Often I sailed toward a patch of wind, only to have it disappear by the time I arrived.

Because of my experience in regatta strategy, I began to sail defensively, but this proved to be the wrong approach. In the critical fifth race, I rounded the leeward mark 10th, and a huge starboard-tack lift came through. In the oscillating wind, it made sense to hang on, even though I was on the outside and losing boats, in the hope that the wind would swing back. As the breeze was shifting inconsistently, the oscillation back was not easy to predict, but this particular shift was strong and long. Major Hall, who eventually won the regatta, took many sterns to sail into the meat of the shift and reaped the rewards. I hung on, but the return oscillation didn't occur until after the finish line.

LESSON: My experience at Devils Lake taught me a tremendous amount about sailing in light air, and provided me with some general rules of thumb. First, patience is a big virtue, and learning to deal with heat and inconsistent conditions can be beneficial. Second, be flexible—committing yourself too soon may be a mistake, and starts should be finalized only at the last possible moment. Third, when a big shift is coming in, sail well into it before tacking. Fourth, be very still in the boat—make only graceful, catlike moves. Fifth, when there is no wind, always aim the boat toward the next mark. And sixth, when sailing upwind, do not allow yourself to stray far from the middle of the course during the first two-thirds of the weather leg.

NEVER SAY DIE

One hundred and three sailors assembled at the ninth World Championships at Ponce, Puerto Rico, for conditions that promised fresh breezes and great surfing waves. In the first race, I got caught outside of a windshift and slipped to 35th place, although I managed to scrape my way back to 11th at the finish. With six races to go, I knew consistent sailing from there on in was a must.

But just before the start of the second race, a boat ran over my transom, pushing me over the starting line early. Circling the committee boat, I had a helpless thought that this series might pose chronic problems and that perhaps I lacked intellectual preparation. But starting last made me aggressive, and I realized flawless sailing was needed. Watching the majority of the fleet go left, I went right—my initial game plan before the start. Rounding the weather mark 15th, I was aware that I had made the big play, and as the race continued, more boats fell behind me. As I sailed up the last weather leg, I thought how much fun sailing is when you are prepared.

LESSON: Winning the second race required patience and concentration, and it proved to me that giving up because of a poor start is a losing attitude.

Twelfth Sunfish Worlds, Sardinia, Italy. (Daniel Forster)

11

Maintenance and Mothering

One of the fathers of the concept of simplicity in the Sunfish class was Jack Evans. As class secretary during the late 1960s and early 1970s, he was the ambassador of true one-design racing. Jack disallowed most everything a sailor might devise to circumvent the rules. The idea, he said, was to get in your boat and sail, not fuss.

During a discussion at a North American Championships, I listened to Jack talk about the Sunfish. He commented that the hull of the boat and its relatively short 14-foot length really did not develop laminar flow, particularly in waves where the boat bounces, causing the bottom flow to become very turbulent. This discussion occurred in an era when sailors dragged their boats across rocks and coral longitudinally, intentionally digging ruts they hoped would improve flow, as do the grooves in a pair of snow skis.

"Just treat the Sunfish as if it was a fourteen-foot boat," Jack said. And as if making a gesture symbolic of his back-to-basics approach, he put his sail numbers on using Roman numerals.

Most good Sunfish sailors adhere to Jack's philosophy of simplicity. Master it, and you can step into any Sunfish and do well. The Sunfish World Championships, where all boats are supplied new from the manufacturer, is a place where this philosophy is put to the test.

THE HULL

One result of the simplicity philosophy is that most boat-related work centers on maintenance rather than on squeezing out a slight edge over competitors. To keep your boat competitive, keep the inside of the hull dry. In heavy seas, or during a capsize, most boats take on some water, which can be absorbed by the fiberglass as well as by the inner foam flotation sections running fore and aft. If left damp, the foam sections can come unglued from the hull, decreasing hull stiffness. Water accumulated in the hull can increase hull weight as much as 20 percent, depending on the amount of water and the length of time it was in the hull. Ideal hull weight is approximately 130 pounds.

Recently, I checked on an old hull I sold to a neighbor. The boat had been neglected, and water had been in the hull for a couple of years as the result of a bow hole. During its prime, the hull weighed 130 pounds, but now it weighed closer to 185 pounds, due to water absorption. Drying the inside of the hull with a heat lamp, and with good air circulation through inspection ports, the boat's weight could be reduced to around 170 pounds. It will never attain its original weight.

There is a hole for hull drainage on the starboard side of the deck. However, drainage from that opening never is complete, and even a cupful of water left in the boat eventually will cause weight gain. The best solution to the problem is to install two six-inch, screw-on inspection ports, which are more watertight than are bayonet inspection ports. The ideal location for the ports is the forward

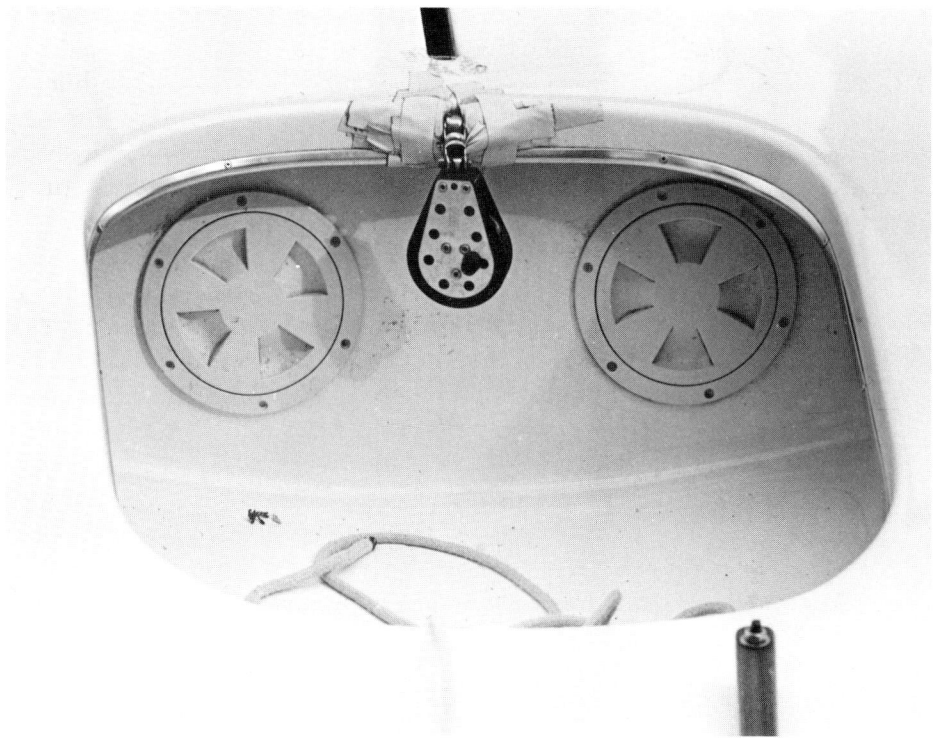

Dual 6-inch inspection ports for easy access. (Bob Pool)

vertical wall of the cockpit. A port on each side of the daggerboard trunk will allow easy access to the hull for sponging, a source of good air circulation for complete drying, and a handy storage place for any extra gear you may need.

When mounting inspection ports, seal the rims with silicone, to ensure they are watertight. This also adds a slight amount of stiffness to the hull. When the boat is not in use, keep the inspection ports open to allow air flow and prevent condensation from building up. Also keep the ports open when transporting the boat on your car, as the warm highway air also does a nice job of drying the hull. Once inspection ports are installed, seal the deck-mounted drain hole with silicone, and don't open it again unless checking for leaks.

To detect leaks, use a vacuum cleaner in reverse, (or a bicycle pump), and some soapy water. First, coat the hull or any suspicious areas with the soapy water. Then remove the deck-mounted drain plug, put the nozzle of the pump or vacuum over the hole and gently force air into the hull. Any leaking sections should cause the soapy water to bubble. To do this properly, you may need two people—one to operate the vacuum cleaner and the other to sponge down the boat and watch for bubbles.

For most hull fittings, the key is cleanliness and ensuring that their fasteners are secure and watertight. At the beginning of every season, take all fittings off, clean them, and put a new layer of silicone on their fasteners. One place to make sure the screws are particularly snug is the halyard cleat, since that cleat does more than one job.

Blasting around downwind can drain your cockpit quickly. Watch to be sure the mainsheet does not get sucked out the bailer. (Bob Pool)

The stock splashboard from the factory is rough and irregular. A thorough sanding will make it fast and effective, eliminating wind and water resistance to some degree. Silicone the entire splashboard and its fasteners in place. If you have an older boat with screws instead of rivets, they too should be sealed.

The bailer is also prone to leakage, so remedy that potential problem by removing it from the hull. This usually requires two people, one to hold the bailer from the bottom of the hull, and one to twist the plastic nut from the cockpit side. With the bailer removed, you might notice slight cracks in the fiberglass around the bailer hole. These can be a source of water seepage, and when reinstalling the bailer, silicone should be liberally applied to that area. To reduce water friction on the bailer, sand it lightly. So that the bailer will be as flush as possible with the bottom of the hull, take the washer that normally fits between the bailer and the hull out and disregard it. Once in place, test the bailer for leakage. If it leaks, try tightening the nut. In some cases, you may be able to solve the problem by applying more silicone.

If you have an old boat with an aluminum bailer, count yourself lucky. They are more efficient and pose less water resistance than do the new plastic bailers. Unlike plastic bailers, the plugs on aluminum bailers are threaded, which allows the plug to be slightly unscrewed, but still functional. The nut on aluminum bailers also can be tightened further than those on the plastic models, and the bailer itself can be sanded lightly to make it less resistant to water flow.

MAINSHEET BRIDLE

One fitting that has undergone a gradual evolution is the mainsheet bridle. For years, the stiff wire bridle was the foundation of all innovation at that end of the boat. In the 1960s, the mainsheet was clipped off on the port side of the bridle loop, which increased performance on starboard tack. In the 1970s, some sailors taped the loop down on the bridle wire, thus creating a "loopless" wire bridle that allowed the mainsheet clip to slide from port to starboard. One of the pioneers of the loopless bridle was Gerrit Zeestraten, who demonstrated it at the 1974 World Championships in Aruba. The only problem arose when the mainsheet clip snagged on the taped-over bridle eye, and time was lost after each tack trying to persuade the sheet to slide to leeward.

Today we have the option of using either a line for the bridle or a standard cable bridle. Most serious racers opt for the line bridle, which allows the mainsheet to slide effortlessly to leeward, as on a Snipe or Laser. However, class rules exclude you from adjusting the bridle tension while sailing. Generally, the bridle is set up tight in heavy winds, no tighter than 30 inches in length to allow the sheet to slide the maximum distance to leeward. In medium winds, the bridle should be about as long as the standard wire bridle. In light air, it should be slightly looser yet. Your tolerance for adjustment is very small. The rule says "31 inches plus or minus one inch." Nevertheless it is worth the trouble.

When rigging a line traveler, use one-quarter-inch, pre-stretched dacron line and tie each end of it to the deck eyes with a bowline. If you are going to be on the water for the entire day and expect the wind velocity to change, carry both the wire bridle and the traveler line with you just in case you want to make a change between races. Keep in mind that the mainsheet should be allowed to slide farther to leeward on starboard tack than on port tack. This will accommodate the difference between the sail's fullness and effectiveness on both tacks. To ensure that the sheet cannot go all the way to the port end of the bridle when on starboard, use the wire bridle and tie the tail to the center loop. This will allow it to slide to leeward on starboard and be centered on port. This is correct for medium winds. (See also page 68.)

Occasionally, you may want the mainsheet set at different positions on the traveler line, such as when sailing in puffy wind conditions. To keep the mainsheet in place once you have positioned it, tape the bridle line with duct tape, then remove the tape. This leaves the bridle line sticky, giving the mainsheet something to stick to. To pull the mainsheet off the area it has adhered to, push on the boom with your feet or hand, then reposition the sheet on the bridle. This gives you the option of a predetermined setting. With the rope bridle this flexibility is impossible.

Last, check the masthole for smoothness. You may have to sand it lightly. If the lip of the deck is not flush with the internal structure of the masthole, sand it flush. If sanding is not adequate, you may need to add silicone as a filler.

THE SPARS

The spars are an often-overlooked item in boat preparation. Spars create an uneven flow of air across the sail, and with the addition of burrs in the aluminum created by rough handling, tape, and unnecessary telltales, the wind flow distortion quickly increases. For that reason, I make sure any burrs are carefully filed off, keep the amount of tape and number of telltales to an absolute minimum, and give each spar a good coat of wax at the beginning of the season.

As with the hull, it is imperative to keep the spars watertight. Water in the spars increases the boat's overall weight, and also soaks into the inner wood cork at the ends of the spars, where it produces a negative effect on the boat's stability.

If you suspect water in the spars, or want to ensure that water never fills the spars, take the plastic end caps off. To do this, remove the tiny pins at the ends of the spar by punching each pin out with a center punch. This drives the pin through the spar and into the plastic cap. If this fails, carefully drill the pin out. Then remove the cap and let the spar dry. When replacing the cap, set it in place with epoxy. For added security, drill another hole on the opposite side of the present boom pin and install an extra pin.

At the 1975 Sunfish Worlds in Miami I didn't have the opportunity to pin the end cap. Winds were light, and I routinely left the halyard loose until eight or nine minutes before the start. When I started to tighten it, the mast cap pulled out and the rig came tumbling down. I was able to tape the mast cap back in place and sail back upwind just in time for the start. Had I been sailing my own boat, which has an extra pin in each cap, the problem never would have occurred.

Another spot to check is the gooseneck. Make sure the brass screw is just loose enough to allow you to slide the gooseneck on the boom. Since it is made of soft metal, use a large screwdriver to adjust it; otherwise you will strip the screw head and the resulting burrs eventually will chafe the sail. To keep the rig closer to the mast, improving pointing ability, the inner nut also should be tightened.

WIND INDICATORS

One of the most variable fittings on the Sunfish is the wind indicator. The range of types and configurations of wind indicators is infinite, and there are a number of things to consider when selecting one. When in close competition with a number of boats, one of the most important factors is durability. It is inevitable that the indicator will get knocked, bumped, hit, and banged while sailing, rigging, or just traveling. A solution is to use indicator arms made of soft aluminum, which, although easily bent, can just as easily be straightened.

In the 1960s, I used a coat hanger taped to the upper booms for a bracket, with a piece of yarn at the end of each arm. But that arrangement bent easily and was difficult to flex back. A recent innovation is the Feathermate, designed by Paul Odegard, who won the 1981 Sunfish North Americans. This design is simple, with flexible arms and relatively low aerodynamics.

The best application of wind indicators is offwind in light air. Unfortunately, under these conditions your body is generally in line with the wind indicator, making it difficult to read accurately, especially if mounted on the leading edge of the upper boom. For a better perspective on that point of sail, a masthead fly is a reasonable alternative. I use a seven-inch piece of small rod with a tiny eyelet on top, taped to the top of the upper boom on the forward side (opposite the outhaul). For the indicator, I use a lightweight strip of colored nylon material.

Like boom-mounted wind indicators, a masthead fly also has its pros and cons. A big plus is that it has only one arm, and since it is up well away from the rig, it is usually a true indicator of wind direction. Another advantage is that, apart from a capsize, it is almost impossible to damage during racing.

However, the masthead fly can be physically tough to read, as continually bending your head back a full 90 degrees is not only awkward, but time consuming. While checking it, you could slam into a wave that will stop your boat, a wave that may have been avoided had you been

1977 Sunfish Worlds in the Bahamas. (Bob Johnstone)

looking ahead rather than up. Frequent checking of the masthead fly also can be an indication to your competition that you are uncertain about your tack or sailing angle. And there are times when your competition will have a better idea about wind direction than you will, just by reading your masthead fly.

Finally, in large swells or in cross-chop, the fly moves erratically, thus becoming virtually useless. When I use a masthead fly, I carry it with me when I leave the beach. If the air is over 12 knots, I don't even attach it to the rig. But if the wind lightens between races I lower the rig and tape the fly in place.

If you decide to use a wind indicator, which the majority of Sunfish sailors do, be careful not to become a slave to it. Some sailors spend too much time watching the indicator instead of observing the wind on the water or preparing tactical decisions. Particularly in heavy air, where the apparent wind and heavy downdrafts make readings inconsistent, wind direction and velocity can just as easily be felt on the body or face. Take the time to study the wind patterns on the water, and you'll probably have a better idea about what's happening on the course than you will if you use the information gained from any one of a number of wind indicators.

When friends or an inexperienced person goes sailing on my boat, I usually take out my old rig. This is an old set of booms with an equally old sail. If the boat is capsized in mud, sand, weeds, or whatever, I have no worries about my racing equipment being damaged. In fact, I even use the old equipment when practicing, especially if I am concentrating more on tactics than on boat speed. An extra rig is a small investment compared to the advantages it provides.

TRANSPORTATION AND STORAGE

Properly transporting the Sunfish also helps ensure a long hull life. The key is never to transport the hull rightside up. Nothing is harder on the hull than the constant vibrations that occur when traveling. Carrying the boat incorrectly just once can greatly harm the stiffness of the fiberglass, and may crack the inner hull foam or cause it to become unglued. When sailing in waves, you can tell which boats have been damaged in this way, for they will pound and reverberate like big kettledrums, sending vi-

The self-sufficient single-handed sailor. (Bob Pool)

brations up through their skippers' spines. Such hulls are fine for recreational use, but will never again attain maximum heavy-air speed.

One of the biggest problems when traveling is getting the boat on a rooftop rack when you have no one to help. To do so, all you need is a stepladder and some padding, such as a towel. Turn the boat upside down, park the car next to it, and set the stepladder up near the bow of the boat. Put the padding on the fourth or fifth ladder step, and lift the bow onto that step. Now lift the stern and pivot the boat around so that you can set the stern up on the racks, being careful not to rotate the boat so far that the bow slips off the step. Then gently lift the bow off the ladder and set the bow up on the rack. This maneuver can be done in reverse to get the boat off the rack, but be careful not to pivot the boat too far, or you

Using a ladder to aid in car-roof transport. (Bob Pool)

will tip the stepladder over.

Winter storage is also an important consideration. As when car-topping, store the hull upside down in a dry location. With the inspection ports left open, the boat will have good air circulation, and the hull should dry thoroughly. If you're short on space, suspend the boat from the ceiling, using wide straps (not rope) to distribute the weight evenly. Another acceptable method is to lean the boat sideways against a wall. Use padding on the floor and on the wall to prevent damage to the hull molding. While the boat is stored, don't allow anything to rest or drip on the bottom.

When storing sails, it is important to prevent wrinkling. Folding the sail produces permanent wrinkles in the cloth, as does leaving the sail on the spar for prolonged periods of time. Remove the sail from the spars and hang it from the tack and clews, if you have the space. A full basement is ideal, although an attic also can be used if the sail is folded in half and hung from the tack, head, and clew. During the summer, when the sail is used with some regularity, leave the sail on the spar and set the spars on end, allowing the sail to hang freely. To do this you need considerable headroom, such as you might have in a garage. Wherever you store your sail, make sure nothing is allowed to sit inside it—especially the family cat.

Store the rudder and daggerboard in a cool, dry place. Suspend them with a piece of line and you should prevent pressure points from developing warpage or cracks.

Adequately preparing your boat is a worthwhile endeavor. You will have accomplished preventive maintenance that will, in turn, provide hassle-free racing. More important, your boat will no longer be an excuse for a poor performance. By the same token, it will no longer be the reason for an exceptional performance, either.

The long upwind leg can take it's toll on unprepared sailors. When sailing an Olympic course the third windward leg can be excruciating. (Bob Pool)

12

The Physical Sunfish Sailor

The world's greatest singlehanded racers of the past few decades are characterized by their great strength and hiking ability. Stories about their incredible conditioning rivals their incredible accomplishments. The late Jeorg Bruder, a tough Brazilian Finn sailor who appeared at the first Sunfish World Championships, carried his Sunfish, completely rigged, to the water's edge—alone! And after a long day of racing, he took it out of the water the same way. Then there's Russian Finn sailor Valentin Mankin, winner of the 1968 Olympic Gold Medal in Finns, who reportedly does twenty-five push-ups with each arm. The stories go on, but the dedication to conditioning that Bruder and Mankin maintained, along with the likes of Paul Elvstrom, Hans Fogh, Peter Barrett, and John Bertrand, has gained them worldwide respect.

Granted, few sailors have the time or energy to devote to training as do these champions, but it is important to practice at least some conditioning. Because singlehanded boats generally sail slower than do larger dinghies and keelboats, speed differences between those at the front of the fleet and those in the middle are not that great. Some attention to conditioning can move you up quickly in the final standings.

In 1972, when I was seventeen, I sailed in the Sunfish Worlds in Bermuda. I was a little timid and anxious about the event because I knew the Bermudan winds are heavy. My suspicions proved correct—the practice race was sailed in winds between 40 and 45 knots. At 160 pounds, I felt a bit inadequate next to the class heavyweights—Bob Bowles and Hans Fogh—for I knew the conditions favored them. Being out-of-shape makes racing no fun.

In the following years, my conditioning program gradually improved, but it was not until the 1975 Worlds that I fully committed myself to a total training program. From November 1974, to April 1975, I trained six days a week. The discipline paid off, and I won that year's Worlds. Ironically, the wind conditions there were relatively light, but the confidence I gained enabled me to sail well in the hot weather.

Much has been written about correct training techniques. However, one thing all training programs seem to lack is a focus on exercises you enjoy doing. Your program should be centered around those exercises. Otherwise, unless you can focus directly on the end product rather than on the means, you'll likely become bored and end your training altogether. I enjoy running and lifting weights, so both have been incorporated into my training. Fortunately, both are great exercises for almost any type of sailing.

Once you have zeroed in on the type of exercise that appeals to you, you must consider your weaknesses. Is it arm strength? Leg strength? Flexibility? In my case, I felt that because sailing is a symmetrical body sport, and because I'm a right hander, the left side of my body needed better conditioning. So I developed a program of exercises that would help me in that area. Eventually, my work enabled me to hike on one leg, regardless of what tack I was on, allowing the other leg to rest from the previous tack. This works only in boats with hiking straps.

HIKING

Because the most physical aspect of Sunfish sailing is hiking, it is important to understand the mechanics of hiking. The favored Sunfish hiking technique is the V-hike. This is the best form for all body types—short, tall, big, small. In a Sunfish, the advantage of this technique is overwhelming because of the boat's lack of hiking straps. With legs spread into a V-shape, more body control is gained over the boat, and instead of exerting all hiking pressure on just one part of your body—such as one foot hooked under the forward edge of the cockpit—the load is now spread over two points. Paul Fendler, who stands only five feet four inches tall and weighs around 135 pounds, used this technique when he won the 1976 Worlds in Venezuela. Even when the wind piped up, he was always with the leaders, hiking hard.

Hiking bench made with less than $20 of material. Can also be used effectively with a water jacket. (Bob Pool)

The Physical Sunfish Sailor · 125

The key to learning good Sunfish hiking technique is to use a hiking bench as a simulator. It's easy and inexpensive to build and, used over the winter, you'll notice big improvements in your hiking stamina the next summer.

As is true of all conditioning techniques, hiking on the bench must be done in sets—a series of repetitions done at differing time intervals. The sets I perform on the bench vary with the conditions I expect to sail in. If I'm going to be sailing on open water with onshore winds and long, moderate puffs, I'll work with a short number of repetitions in long sets. If I'll be sailing in offshore breezes or where there are short, hard puffs, as on a lake, I'll do shorter sets with a larger number of repetitions. Always, I aim first for quality, than quantity.

When working on the hiking bench, I start six months prior to a major event. Such conditioning builds up muscle groups and cardio-vascular endurance, and takes time to produce results. Before any workout, always stretch each muscle group carefully. This helps avoid injury when performing the actual exercises and increases flexibility.

During most workouts, I divide my time into three parts, running, weights, and rest. I perform flexibility and weight exercises on Mondays, Wednesdays and Fridays, and run on Tuesdays, Thursdays and Saturdays. I maintain this schedule from Thanksgiving until Easter, when I can't sail because of cold weather.

Any workout should include up to 80 percent isotonic exercises, which build cardiovascular endurance. Do exercises in sets, with a minimum of three repetitions of each set—and preferably 10 to 15 repetitions. For example, if you are doing a set of forward leg curls, your routine might be:

1. warm-ups—30 pounds: 10 repetitions
2. set 1—50 pounds: 15 repetitions
3. set 2—60 pounds: 15 repetitions
4. set 3—70 pounds: 10 repetitions
5. set 4—70 pounds: 15 repetitions

Heavy air work downwind can be physically demanding. Oftentimes more so than heavy air upwind. (Bob Pool)

Once the sets are complete, move on to an exercise that focuses on another muscle group. Rotate sets between lower and upper body muscles to allow each area of your body to rest during set breaks.

One of the best methods of ensuring quality workouts is to closely monitor your activity through predicted maximal heart rate (P.M.H.R.). This system allows adjustment for age and lets you know when you are making cardio-vascular gains. The formula is 220 minus your age equals P.M.H.R. If your age is 30, your P.M.H.R. is 190 heart beats per minute. During a workout to make cardio-vascular gains, your heartbeat should fall within 70 to 80 percent of that number, between 133 and 152 beats per minute. The best time to take your pulse is immediately after finishing a workout. As your fitness improves, you

Running on edge. (Bob Pool)

will notice it takes more effort to get your pulse up to the 70-percent minimum, and you should feel a sense of accomplishment, because you are gaining on the cardiovascular needs of your body.

There are many variations of the ideal workout program. Many people prefer to substitute a game or sporting event for workouts, such as racquetball, squash, tennis, handball, hockey, or swimming. This is acceptable as long as the exercise is undertaken for at least sixty minutes. Otherwise it will be difficult for you to make the necessary gains.

When racing, you must always be ready and able to make split-second decisions while maintaining balance and trim. Fatigue results in poor decisions that will impair these essential elements. To ensure all energy is put to optimum use, strength, flexibility, and endurance is a necessity.

Three contrasting sailing outfits: foul-weather gear, one-piece sailing suit, and wet suit.

13

Garments For Speed

The trend in small-boat racing is to keep the body functioning at maximum efficiency at all times. Just as no high-caliber runner would consider racing in shoes not specifically tailored to his needs, no quality sailor should consider racing in clothes that prevent him from performing at peak level.

Whenever your body under- or overheats, added stress results in mental or physical mistakes. If you're not dressed appropriately for the conditions, it is likely you will falter. Other clothing factors to be considered, besides warmth and coolness, are weight, particularly when wet, and the amount of flexibility the garment affords. The choice obviously depends on the sailing conditions.

In light winds, air temperature is usually warm, if not down right hot. Select light-colored clothing that is loose fitting. If the wind is less than 10 knots and the air warm, I do not wear shoes, for feet can act as an important sensory tool. If there is enough air to allow me to sit on the deck, I place my forward foot on the cockpit floor at the point of the forward curve on the vertical cockpit wall, and place my aft foot flat in the middle of the cockpit. With both feet I can feel the flow around the board and along the bottom of the boat. Particularly after a tack, the sensations and vibrations provide me with information about my speed. I object to wearing shoes in these conditions because they tend to soak up water dripping from my pants from roll-tacking and jibing and become added weight.

One factor to consider is that offwind, when sailing at about the same speed as the wind, your body heats up considerably. For this reason, I dress on the cool side. Any body movement used upwind usually helps keep me warm there. However, if you have problems with strains or muscle pulls, dress on the warm side.

In heavy air, clothing adds important weight to your body. However, it must still allow you flexibility, comfort, and warmth. One of the best heavy-air articles of clothing is a one-piece dinghy suit. This meets all heavy-air requirements except weight, and if desired, this can be achieved by wearing wet sweatshirts or a water jacket.

Another heavy-air essential is a good pair of padded hiking pants or shorts. Hiking on the sharp deck edge reduces circulation to the lower legs. When that blood flow is restricted, lactic acid quickly builds up. This is what causes the sensation of muscle fatigue and leg cramps, destroying concentration and the ability to think rationally in difficult situations. There are many versions of padded hiking pants, but the key is to use whatever keeps you most comfortable, allows the greatest flexibility, and is not excessively heavy when wet. A simple alternative is to wear several pairs of shorts made of thick material. If you find your hiking pants tend to slide down when you hike, wear suspenders, which also help transfer strain on the hips to the shoulders.

Water jackets are one of the more controversial items in small-boat sailing. There's no question they can increase speed in a breeze, but there's concern about how they affect the back. The key to staying healthy while wearing a water jacket is to train well in advance and

One-piece spray suit over water jacket with two full bottles. (Lee Parks)

work slowly into it, wearing a little more weight each time. Wearing the jacket while dry-land training, either working out on a hiking bench or running, helps build your back muscles. Be sure to stretch prior to wearing the jacket so your muscles are warmed up.

The first time you wear a water jacket, you may experience some difficulty. Water jackets do not fit well, and if you have large neck muscles or rounded shoulders, they tend to slide off. If so, have elastic bands sewn across the chest and back of the jacket by a local sailmaker or cobbler. Wearing slippery nylon jackets or shirts underneath the water jacket also causes it to shift around. A good half-sleeve sweatshirt will reduce shifting.

Another problem with water jackets is that they impair mobility, strength, and stamina. If you are just beginning to use the jacket, you may feel some numbness, along with a top-heavy sensation. If you reach that point, the jacket should be removed. Go back and train some more, or reduce the amount of weight you carry until you feel more secure and confident. With plenty of practice and common sense, using the jacket can be safe and easy.

One advantage of the water jacket is its ability to hold water of different temperatures. If it's a cold, windy day, fill the jacket with hot water, and it will act as a fine body insulator. This is especially helpful after the first race, or after lunch, when you start cooling off and your muscles begin to tighten. Remember, maximum weight for all clothing following a one-minute draining period, is, by class rules, 22 pounds (10 kilos).

Although it does not greatly help your performance, one of the most important pieces of clothing is a life jacket. It should be snug-fitting. If you have problems with the mainsheet hanging up on the back of the jacket, wear a T-shirt over it. If you are confident in your sailing and swimming ability, and if the rules permit, it may be helpful to remove the life jacket in light air, making your body less wind resistant and increasing your flexibility.

Remember, the sailing garment may be as important as any other boat-speed ingredient. Maintain a no-nonsense approach, avoiding hoods, extra pockets, and other nonessentials. Other than that, the key in clothing selection is comfort. If you're not comfortable, you're not going to perform well. It's as simple as that.

14

The Clubhouse

Sunfish racers are a unique breed of sailors. The diversity of age and personality make it a truly remarkable class. Having sailed in other popular single-handed classes, I find the Sunfish is the friendliest and most fun-loving group. It is the grass roots of single-handed board-boat sailing. To continue its success in decades to come, we must nurture that spirit and especially encourage novices in the class. Making the novice feel at home and helping him learn to race is sportsmanlike; intimidating beginners on the water is unjust and irrational. The overwhelming spirit should be that sailing involves friendly competition. We are dealing with a series of complex variables. Learning to make sense and order out of these variables is really fun. And sailing within the confines of the racing game is the ultimate in sailing enjoyment.

Fortunately for everyone, sailing can be a lifetime hobby. Sailing a boat that fits your age and ability can mean a lifelong racing career. Few sports offer this kind of extended pleasure.

The Clubhouse is where the action is put into words, and where sometimes, the words put into action. Sailors are people with many fine attributes. There is seldom a sport where information about strategy and technique flows so freely and openly. There is much to learn from each other. Ask the winners and losers to explain certain moves or adjustments made on the water. Watch them rig their boats and pack their cars and try their methods youself. If something does not work, make a note and discard it. No two people sail the boat exactly the same way, but we are all playing the same game.

15

Appendix

One of the best ways to thoroughly prepare for a regatta is to use a regatta checklist. Oftentimes sailors become rushed prior to leaving and forget something important. A list is helpful.

SAILING GEAR:

Sail
Upper and lower booms
Rudder, with extension
Daggerboards
Mast
Inspection ports
Bailer plug
Halyard
Sheets: 1 light air, 1 medium air, 1 heavy air
Telltales
Foul weather gear
Sail suit

Hiking shorts
Water jacket
Life jackets
Hiking shoes and/or boots
Gloves
Sponge
Rule book and appeals books
Sunfish class rules
Notetaking notebook
Hat
Tape
2 starting watches
Sandpaper of all grades
Portable screwdriver and pliers
Drinking bottle

SUPPORT GEAR

Toolbox
Rivet gun with stainless steel rivets
Extra ⅛ inch dacron line
Tape measure
Oversized screwdriver
Silicone seal
Extra sail sets
Screws and bolts, brass or stainless
Marine tex or micro-balloons
Mat or padding, to place your boat on an irregular beach
Extra boom blocks
Extra deck block
Extra eye straps
Extra bridle, rope or wire

RACING PIE GRAPH

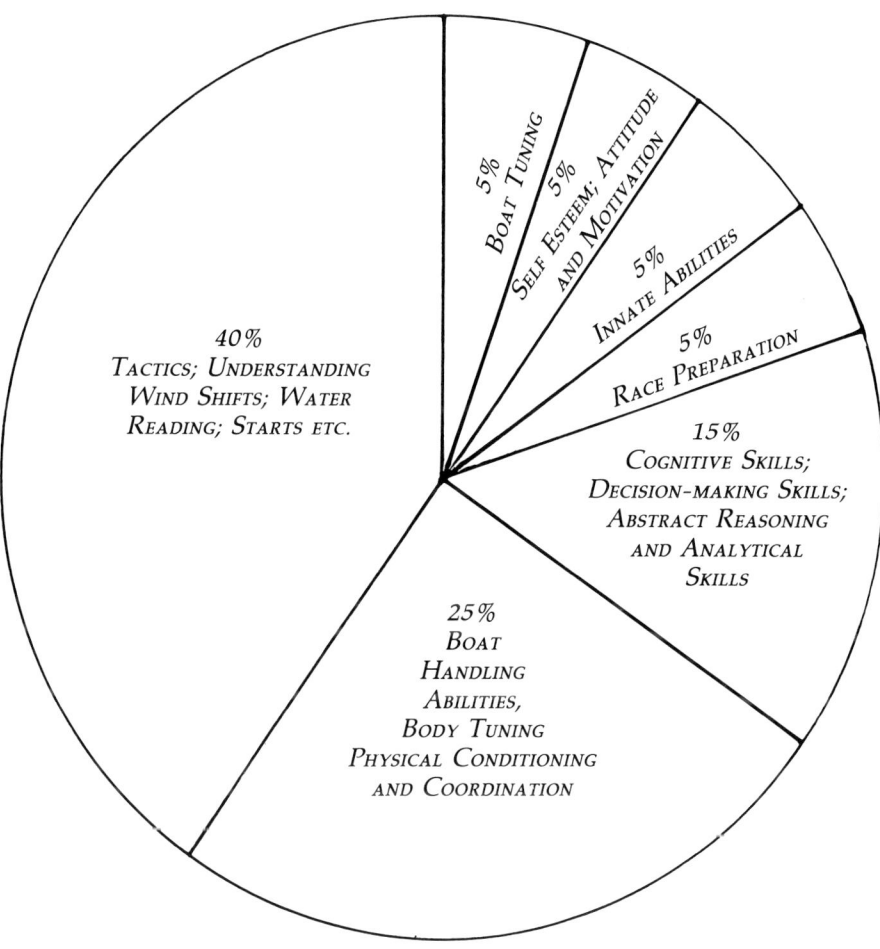

The racing pie provides a systematic breakdown of the general racing prerequisites. This is specifically designed for the Sunfish with a premium placed on physical conditioning and tactics.

Regatta Note Sheet

When a race or regatta ends, much has been learned and enjoyed. The exposure to many different techniques and situations provide experience that should not go to waste. It's not surprising, then, that some of the world's greatest sailors make a habit of jotting down notes after each event, giving them a lifelong log of information that might otherwise have been forgotten. Remembering a particular facet of a regatta site may be difficult without notes, and if you're likely to sail there again, ten minutes to fill out a note sheet is a small investment to help ensure good performance the next time you race.

Date_____

Wind Direction_____

Wind Speed_____   Boat_____

Temp._____   Time_____

Skies_____   Waters_____

Regatta_____Drill_____   Current_____

Results_____

A. Positive Input:

   1.

   2.

   3.

   4.

   5.

   6.

B. Negative Input:

   1.

   2.

   3.

   4.

   5.

Diagrams on back

Sunfish World Championship
Ponce, Puerto Rico

Date **3/4-12/78**
Wind Direction **S.E.**
Wind Speed **10 mph to 40 mph**   Boat **#988**
Temp. **85° - 90°**   Time
Skies **P. Cloudy**   Waters **Atlantic**
Regatta **✓** Drill   Current **0 - 0⁺**
Results **1st World Champion**

Race #1   #2   #3   #4   #5   #6
      17   0   11   3   (18) 0
      11   1st   6   2   (12) 1st

A. Positive Input:

1. Good behavior and style. Cool and Calm.
2. Good Tactics (Great Upwind) = Open Seas, Steady Air
3. 75% races correct to go to semi-laylines upwind
4. Good ability to think all winter long about tactics and sailing. Previous results were clear in mind.
5. Good concentrative sailing definitely worth investment.
6. Very good pre-race goals and decisions.

B. Negative Input:

1. Middle of line sag does not start until middle of line
2. Learn to compensate for wave and wind drift on starting line.
3.
4. In the 5th race when only 4.3 pts. ahead of Pierre S., made a mistake at the start. Ended up in middle of the line. Should have done 1 of 2 things.
5. 1) Either stayed much closer to Pierre S. or,
    2) Gone with own Game Plan. Probably with lead, should have gone with #2, because
Diagrams on back   I knew right side was favored more than left.

UPWIND SAIL ADJUSTMENTS
(FOGH SAIL)

Sail Control	Drifter 0-3	Light Wind 3-5	Medium 5-10	Heavy 10-6	Heavy 15+
Sheet	Medium-tight	Medium-tight	Tight	Near two-blocked	Near two-blocked
Bridle	Center	Center	Slid off to port-3"	Slid all the way off on port	Slid all the way off on port and starboard
Downhaul	Loose	Loose	Loose upwind; medium-tight downwind	Loose upwind-tight downwind	Tight all points of sail
Upper Outhaul	Medium-loose 5"	Loose 7"	Medium-loose 5"	Tight 3"	Very tight 2"
Lower Outhaul	Loose 7"	Loose 7"	Medium-loose 5"	Medium-loose 4"	Very tight 3"
Gooseneck	17½"	17½"	18½"	19"	20"-21"

Index

AMF Alcort, 27

bailer, 113
Barrett, Peter, 51, 123
Barrett start, 51
Barrington board, 28–33
Bertrand, John, 123
boom vang, 13–15
Bowles, Bob, 102, 104, 124
Bruder, Jeorg, ix, 123
by-the-lee, 83–4, 89

Catalano, Mike, 79
Championship of
 Championships, 4
 1982 Rush Creek, Texas, 53–4
Chapin, Dave, ix, 17, 20
checklist, 137
Christianson, John, 11
daggerboard, 27, 66–67
 storage, 121

downwind sailing, 83–89
 light air, 85–6
 heavy air, 86–7

Ehman, Tom, 104
Elvstrom, Paul, 123
Evans, Jack, 102, 109–10

"fat board," 30, 31
Fendler, Paul, 25, 125
Fogh, Hans, ix, 123–24
Fogh sail, 15, 18
Force 5, 1
Friend, Chris, 82

garments, 131–4
gooseneck, 2, 13, 14
Greater Detroit Sunfish Regatta, 59
Griffin, Dick, 104–5

Hall, Major, ix, 104, 106
helm, *see* rudder,
hiking, 63–5, 125–6, 132
Hookanson, Jens, 17
Hoyt, Gary, ix
hull care, 110–13, 118–21

inspection ports, 110–11
IYRU rules, x, 78

JC strap, 11–12
Jens rig, 17–24
Jobson, Gary, ix

Klinger, Kerry, 34
Knight, Carl, ix, 28–30, 104–5
Kostecki, John, 10

Laser, 1, 4, 114
leaks, 112
leech control, 9–11
Lewis, Larry, 104
Lihan, Tom, 4

mainsheet bridle, 68, 113–15, 143
Mankin, Valentin, 123
mark roundings, 87–9
Millican, Chuck, 104
Moore, Ted, 104–5

notetaking, 103–4, 140–1
North American Sunfish Championship:
  1970 Winnetka, Ill., 104
  1971 Sayville, N.Y., 101–2

1973 Devil's Lake, Mich. 105–6
1976 Association Island, N.Y., 17

Odegard, Paul, 116
outhauls, 5–9
Owen, Jim, 84

physical conditioning, 123–29
planing, 76–9
predicted maximal heart rate (P.M.H.R.), 127

Ratsey sail, 15
reach, 73–81
roll-jibe, 91, 96–100
roll-tack, 91–5
rudder, 27–8, 33–5, 73–5,
  storage, 121

sails, 1–15
  storage, 121
Scott, Manton, ix
Siegentheler, Pierre, 67
splashboard, 113
Snipe, 114
spar maintenance, 115–16
starts, 47–55, 107
  Barrett start, 51
  favored end, 48, 55
  warning signal, 49
steering, body, 75, 84
storage, 121

telltale, *see* wind indicator,
Timme Angsten Regatta, 103
transportation, 118–21

upwind sailing, 57–71
  light air, 58–61
  medium and heavy air, 61–6

water jackets, 132–4
White, Will, ix, 104
wind, 37–45
wind indicators, 116–18
  Feathermate, 116
World Sunfish Championship:
  1972 Bermuda, 124
  1973 Martinique, 67
  1974 Aruba, 114
  1975 Miami, 124
  1976 Venezuela, 125
  1977 Nassau, 46, 117
  1978 Puerto Rico, 11, 34, 48, 67, 107
  1980 Aruba, 75
  1981 Sardinia, 36, 108

Zeestraten, Gerrit, 114